NON-CONCEPTUAL NEGATIVITY

BEFORE YOU START TO READ THIS BOOK, take this moment to think about making a donation to punctum books, an independent non-profit press,

@ https://punctumbooks.com/support/

If you're reading the e-book, you can click on the image below to go directly to our donations site. Any amount, no matter the size, is appreciated and will help us to keep our ship of fools afloat. Contributions from dedicated readers will also help us to keep our commons open and to cultivate new work that can't find a welcoming port elsewhere. Our adventure is not possible without your support.

Vive la Open Access.

Fig. 1. Hieronymus Bosch, *Ship of Fools* (1490–1500)

NON-CONCEPTUAL NEGATIVITY: DAMAGED REFLECTIONS ON TURKEY. Copyright © 2019 Zafer Aracagök. This work carries a Creative Commons BY-NC-SA 4.0 International license, which means that you are free to copy and redistribute the material in any medium or format, and you may also remix, transform and build upon the material, as long as you clearly attribute the work to the authors (but not in a way that suggests the authors or punctum books endorses you and your work), you do not use this work for commercial gain in any form whatsoever, and that for any remixing and transformation, you distribute your rebuild under the same license. http://creativecommons.org/licenses/by-nc-sa/4.0/

Originally published as *Kavramsız Negativite: Adorno+Hayat+Deleuze* (Istanbul: Sub Press, 2017)

English translation by author published in 2019 by dead letter office, BABEL Working Group, an imprint of punctum books, Earth, Milky Way. https://punctumbooks.com

The BABEL Working Group is a collective and desiring-assemblage of scholar–gypsies with no leaders or followers, no top and no bottom, and only a middle. BABEL roams and stalks the ruins of the post-historical university as a multiplicity, a pack, looking for other roaming packs with which to cohabit and build temporary shelters for intellectual vagabonds. We also take in strays.

ISBN-13: 978-1-950192-03-8 (print)
ISBN-13: 978-1-950192-04-5 (ePDF)

DOI: 10.21983/P3.0247.1.00

LCCN: 2018968575
Library of Congress Cataloging Data is available from the Library of Congress

Book design: Vincent W.J. van Gerven Oei
Cover image: Zafer Aracagök, "Last Vestiges of Oh Horse Me Please, Turkey," watercolor, acrylic, pen, pencil, 15 × 20 cm, 2016.

All artworks by the author.

HIC SVNT MONSTRA

ZAFER ARACAGÖK

NON-CONCEPTUAL NEGATIVITY
DAMAGED REFLECTIONS ON TURKEY

Ⓟ

CONTENTS

Foreword by Franco Berardi • xiii

Author's Preface: An Imaginary Report
from a Victim of Neanderthal Capitalism • xvii

★

Divergent • 23
Nano-Fascism • 24
Desire Production Zero • 25
Figure • 26
Hetero-Power-Rat • 27
Capitalism, Neanderthalism, and the Despot • 28
Orientalism • 30
Confession • 31
Boredom • 33
Paradoxical Element • 34
Un-Mimetic • 36
Hegel-Nano-Organism • 37
Neanderthal Manifesto • 38
Torn to Pieces But Still Standing • 40
Suicide Bomber • 41
Macro/Micro/Nano-Fascism • 42
Romanticism • 44
Now • 47
The Subject • 49
Somnambulist Situationists • 50
Wish • 52
Representation • 53
When Will They Come to an End? • 55
In Memoriam: Ulus Baker • 56
The Thing • 58
Pessimism • 59
Schizo-Incest • 61
Application • 62
Plato, Mimesis, Coup d'état • 63
The Figure • 64
Aufhebung in Reverse • 65
The King-Fish • 66
White Noise • 67
Maps and Coordinates • 69
Aporia • 70
The Artwork • 71

Negation of Negation vs.
    Affirmation • 72
Project • 75
Castrators of Desire • 77
Michael Kohlhaas • 78
Neanderthal Rationality • 81
Literature • 82
The Dream • 85
Bartleby • 86
Onto-Terrorism • 87
Sculpture • 89
Birds, Horses, Insects… • 91
"Philosopher" • 92
Negotiations • 94
Economy, Capital, and
    Rape • 95
Children • 97
Photograph • 99
Old Age • 101
Negativity • 102
Cutupidité • 103

Animals • 105
Champions of
    Affirmation • 107
Partisans • 108
Metaphysics • 109
Stupidity • 110
Zombie-Art • 111
Mimesis • 113
Adorno: *Negative
    Dialectics* • 114
Laughter • 117
New Year • 118
Shock: 2017 • 119
Antidote • 120
Caravaggio • 121
Repetition • 123
Surrender • 125
Somnambulist Situationist
    Manifesto • 126
Non-Conceptual
    Negativity • 127

★

Bibliography • 131

Dedicated to the memories of those who were murdered, injured, and put under arrest in Gezi uprisings in Istanbul 2013.

FOREWORD

Franco Berardi

When I read (is reading the right action to do in a case like this?), when I browsed (is browsing the action?), when I smelled, touched and perused Zafer's book entitled *I Want to be a Suicide Bomber,* I got the feeling of a malicious sympathy.

The would be suicidal bomber is a semiotic transformer: no more fear, no more hatred, no more humiliation or subjection. Just lines of escape from the terrorist forms of life that we are obliged to witness in the normal streets of the normal world every normal day. Just lines of escape from the daily suicide that is called salaried labor, family life, and accumulation of something.

The suicide bomber is back, now, and is trying to understand how many layers of Fascism have been laid down on our skin, on our city, on the air that we breathe.

Fascism in fact comes in layers, in sheets, in blankets covering every pore of our skin up to the point of transforming our body (and our soul) into a stiffened armor, simultaneously protective and suffocating.

The word Fascism comes from the Italian word *fascio,* which means a bundle, a stack: the unified and narrow identification of different units: human beings uniformed and assimilated: populist identification of singularities into uniformity.

Salaried labor and normalized sexuality, the abolition of sensibility.

But Zafer speaks of nano-fascism. What does it mean?

Nano-fascism is the result of a process of inoculation of the semiotic code of discourtesy (the inmost feature of Fascism) into the fabric of daily life.

Courtesy is the cultural elaboration of the sexual instinct (which obviously does not exist). This culturalization enabled modern civilization. Courtesy is the enticement, and refinement (but simultaneously imbrication and bridling) of sexual desire and also of the other dimensions of social intercourse (they usually say: inter-action).

Certainly we live in a time of the eclipsing of courtesy, almost a time of disappearance of the pleasure of talking and touching and smiling.

So people run into fascism and they do not even know that this is the source of their coarseness and of their unhappiness.

Metropolitan dwellers are in a rush, in a race, in a permanent competition to survive.

Discourtesy is the defining trait of contemporary citizenship. Nano-fascism is the viral device that promotes and inoculates discourtesy.

Modern civilization was based on the humanization of the animal instinct.

The domestication of sex by language, the transformation of urge into desire, is linguistic effect. From the Arab world, from the poetry of Ibn Hazm and the thought of Ibn Arabi, a flow of courtesy streams all along the Mediterranean coast. From Northern Africa to Sicily, from Spain to Catalonia, to Provence, to Tuscany, a number of poets and minstrels calling themselves troubadours are roaming and visiting the castles and the mansions of the late Middle Age's seigneurs. Courtesy does not mitigate desire, but translates attraction into words, images, and spiritual suggestions.

Dolce stil novo (Dante, Cavalcanti, Guinizzelli) is the poetical movement that changes the perception of the erotic other. Beatrice (the woman who gives beatitude) is a sign of the infinite magnificence of the creation of god and the source of the intellectual pleasure which is the condition of erotic joy.

But courtesy was only a stream of the huge river of modernity. Modern history has been a long fight between two tendencies: the erotic play of bodies searching for pleasure and harmony, and the violent uniformity of bodies in the domain of labor, war, and patriarchal submission.

A few decades ago, courtesy was dismissed and almost ridiculed for the sake of unrelenting competition. The neoliberal cult of competition obliterates the space of sensuousness from the social sphere, then connectivity cancels the space of ambiguity, and irony. Cynicism is the formatted language of the economic exchange that implies the end of courtesy, while advertising is the manipulation of courtesy and the cynical replacement of courtesy with permanent hypocrisy.

Pleasure replaced by commodity, courtesy replaced by manipulation: this is the effect of neoliberal capitalism, and the obfuscation of courtesy, and the oblivion of the erotic dimension of language.

Cynical humans know that things are free, and that man is unfree. Man has to subordinate himself to the needs of the thing, to the disposition of technology. When this does not occur and man acts freely, this is a failure from the point of view of the general economy, of effectiveness.

From the point of view of the effective economy men fail when they behave in an intrinsically human manner.

Queer is the ineffective side of energy, the ineffective dissipation of energy.

"Queer is the now of the past unfulfilled promises of the future." (Zafer).

The disappearing of courtesy is the beginning of micro-Fascism. The language of discourtesy is the production of nano-fascist memes.

Did I read the Zafer's book in a proper way?

— January 2018

AUTHOR'S PREFACE

AN IMAGINARY REPORT FROM A VICTIM OF NEANDERTHAL CAPITALISM

With all my production of literature, philosophy, music, and art since 1994, I have tried to conjure up various strategies to fight the rising tide of fascism and racism but especially the single-minded ways of being and thinking which have become the major trend in Turkey and all the world during the last four decades. This trend has grown into a particular case between 2002 and 2018 in Turkey with the aid of American and European manipulations which I have named "nano-fascism" and "Neanderthal capitalism" in my recent works. The idea of Neanderthal capitalism is the result of the proliferation of populist governments and leaders which has flourished all across Europe and America in the name of making these countries "strong again." This common will which has been adopted by the masses has ended up in the election of the world's most violent and greediest political leaders and is built on a limitless desire of a neanderthal violence structured on the endless appropriation of anything that stretches between oneself and the horizon. It is more than rendering everything to be identical with one's own desire (as, say, in Adorno and Horkheimer's *Dialectic of Enlightenment*) as the desire itself is now relocated and reidentified as the crypt of a long-lost atopology within the psyche, thus making even the process of identification unnecessary. When identification once required at least the availability of two separate things, with the rise of the Neanderthal capitalism, the unity or the inseparability of the identifier and the identified is overdetermined at birth with the production of those subjects whose inclusion of all the universe within themselves as "one" will lead to a perennial violence and fight against the ones who do not obey this rule. This sounds like reverting back to primitive roots but only with the exception of what I have called "nano-fascism." The latter could be invented only in the post-capitalist era as a result of a massive stupification of the in-dividual for whom there is no difference between the mediated and the media. The in-dividual of nano-fascism, in its difference from macro- and micro-fascism, has no notion of fascism as it steps into the world with chips of fascism integrated into it via socio-nano-technologies of the psyche and the body. The in-dividual of Neanderthal capitalism is born a fascist with all its cells infused with the minutest details of how to fight and destroy each other for an unquenchable desire to have the upper hand over one another with an eye to perfect integrity and discipline — the murder and death of anything that pertains to life, as it were. In contrast to Leibnizian monadology where each monad includes in itself all the universe, the nano-fascist thinks the whole universe is included only within itself and anything against this rule can be the initiator of the most violent acts, even against the rebellious nano structures within his own physical and psychological make-up.

Without doubt for this schema to be realised, the West had to wait for some results to be obtained from a laboratory country which is called Turkey. The Turkish political scene has always been designed by Western hands but the period between 2002 and 2018 deserves a special attention as Turkey has seen the rise of Neanderthal capitalism and nano-fascism to its fullest capacity. First, Islam. Among all the monotheist religions, Islam is the only one where the schizophrenic schema which is the base of all religions is denied to the extent of making not only the believer but also the deity the victim of a unity as one side of the same coin. The schizophrenic in the first place requires a space, a distance from the other with whom it will put itself into a relative relationship in a manner of rupture and worship. The transcendental must keep itself distant from the worshipper to yield either to belief or disbelief, but this distance is an absolute necessity for the schizophrenic to come alive. In contrast, this distance is abolished in Islam and the believer and the believed or the worshipper and the worshipped are already identified with each other (in accordance with the neanderthal logic), and they occupy the same side of the coin, leaving the other side to be a place without an occupant, that is, a realm of the voice of the symbolic father, from the yoke of which neither Allah nor the worshipper is free: "Ikra" (or: Read!). Mohammed does not read but is read by this command—a perfect subject of *enunciation*. This very same side then turns into a place waiting for its occupant, that is, the place of the would-be dictator who will occupy it as the occupant with no place, as an empty transcendental. The dictator will thus ensure his power over the two by being both the occupant with no place and the resident of the place with no occupant by the displacement of the transcendental. Conceptually speaking, this is where nothing will transcend the conceptual unity of the worshipper and the worshipped except the voice of the dictator who will be incessantly reading and conceptualising the two. One side occupied by a *transcendental* which does not transcend and the other with an *empty transcendental* as an absolute transcender. Worshipper and the worshipped on one side, and the voice of the dictator, on the other. Having erased the schizophrenia of the me and the other with the unity of the worshipper and the worshipped, this is where the capitalism turns into Neanderthal capitalism. If the outcome of this project is nano-fascism—that is, the incorporation of the empty transcendental by the worshipper and the worshipped who do not know what identification is—such a moment also signals the birth of a special clinical case, namely, Cotard's delusion.[1] "Being the sub-ject that I am, I knew that I've

---

[1] "One of the strangest and rarest mental disorders that has been studied academically is Cotard's Syndrome (CS), and also known as the Cotard Delusion, the Nihilistic Delusion, and the Walking Corpse Syndrome, CS is where individuals hold the delusional belief that they are dead (figuratively or literally) and do not exist. [...] CS is named after the 19th-century French neurologist Jules Cotard who first described the condition in 1880. Cotard named the disorder the 'negation delirium' (*le délire de négation*)" (Mark

always been dead!" This is why the growing number of suicide bombers has invaded not only the Middle-East but will soon invade the whole world, given the growing tendency to appropriate the desire to erase the distinction between the identifier and the identified. Leibniz's monad had no windows but the victim of the Cotard's delusion does not even know what a window is.

The worshipper is thus doubly negated first by the Allah who refuses to separate itself from the worshipper and then by the voice of the dictator: "You are no one without me and I am no one without the dictator!" The result is no more the schizo of late capitalism but the doubly negated, and hence affirmed and integrated, nano-fascist of Neanderthal capitalism. "Everything must be included in me as unseparated and undifferentiated, otherwise I kill you and if not I kill myself." Such is the motto of the nano-fascist under the aegis of Neanderthal capitalism.

It comes as no surprise, then, when the results obtained from a laboratory called Turkey are applied to the Western countries (among whom America is the prime example), the expectation is that it will yield to the same Cotard's delusion as a total submission of the subject to the voice of the dictator in order to be negated. The novelty of nano-fascism is that it does not ask for obedience any more, but is more a matter of letting oneself be read and conceptually negated by the dictator, that is, agreeing to be dead. Yes, there is no Hitler today but in the absence of Nietzsche or Schlegel brothers, nobody in the West is ready to accept this (except, perhaps, the followers of Marquis De Sade) as a matter of fact. The sadist, as Deleuze put it, will never reach a full satisfaction unless everything in the world is destroyed. It is already there in Joy Division's album cover "Closer" in 1980. All the tracks from "Still" (1981) are particular symptoms of approaching Cotard's delusion: to be dead. The latter was once adopted as a strategical tool of the Punk: it was actually the core of Punk — how to enjoy the death disco under the deprived cir-

---

D. Griffiths, "Dead Strange: A Beginner's Guide to Codard's Syndrome," *Psychology Today*, October 14, 2014, https://www.psychologytoday.com/us/blog/in-excess/201410/dead-strange).

cumstances. However, within twenty years this strategy, adopted by Neanderthal capitalism, turned into how to make the masses know no difference between the identifier and the identified. The nano-fascist as a dead body is now devouring everything that lies outside his horizon, that is everything which raises the problem of identification. Everything should appear without appearing as something already identified and dead. The situation is no different than the one described by Roger Caillois: what was once considered a radical move is now reverted to the subjection of the masses to the desire of melting into the background, thus, forgetting the categories of time and space which were the sole conditions of the subject to appear as such. Neanderthal capitalism, backed up by Islamic dogma, is now the real enemy. How to appropriate the negative? A nonconceptual negativity is extremely difficult under these circumstances, but not impossible.

The nonconceptual in fact is the residue of Neanderthal capitalism because whatever it appropriates in the name of a monadology (which doesn't even know what a window is) is prone to get lost within the atopology of the surface as the unmaintable. The nonconceptual therefore is not the opposite of the conceptual but that which is always already yet to come. Imagine, for example, Ian Curtis sang his songs always from within a coffin and when he committed suicide, he was already dead. The double negative at work here is not there to affirm the death-affirming voice of the Dictator but to negate radically what is being imposed on us as conceptual and affirmative.

Please don't die.

DIVERGENT

In the spring of 1799, the 21-year-old Kleist wrote a letter to his half-sister Ulrike in which he found it "incomprehensible how a human being can live without a plan for his life [*Lebensplan*]."[1]

On November 21, 1811, the very same Heinrich von Kleist shot his beloved, the terminally ill Henriette Vogel, and then himself, on the banks of Kleiner Wannsee. The innkeeper who housed them the night before described the couple, thirty-four and thirty-one, as cheerful and voluble; Kleist wrote in a final letter to his sister that he viewed death with "inexpressible serenity."

---

[1] Heinrich von Kleist, *The Marquise of O— and Other Stories,* ed. and trans. David Luke and Nigel Reeves (New York: Penguin Books, 1978), 7.

NANO-FASCISM

Nano-fascism is distinguished from micro-fascism in the sense that it is not based on mimesis. In micro-fascism, there is still a figure (or rather, a model), and the subject constructions are maintained on the basis of whether this figure/model is imitated and thus interiorized. In nano-fascism there is neither a figure nor a model left; following a biological mutation, all the specifications that go into the making of a fascist come ready-at-hand in a box, and after a certain period of incubation, they permeate the body down to all of its nano-units.

DESIRE PRODUCTION ZERO

Micro-politics is — in the first place — activated via emancipation of the body. Desire production knows nothing about the erogenous zones; traversing the surface of the body without organs at each point and instant, it triggers the *clinamen*[1] in each atom. The body owes its emancipation to this fact and the thought cannot become what it is not without this movement. Therefore, the reason for the violence suffered at the borders today can be found in the investment of the energies of all the masses whose desire production is emptied down to zero level with the body without organs lowered down to nought and deprived of the animate/inanimate distinction in becoming-destructive.

---

1   As explained by Lucretius in his *De Rerum Natura (The Nature of Things)*, trans. David R. Slavitt (Berkeley: University of California Press, 2008) and in one of the appendices Deleuze wrote for his *The Logic of Sense*, trans. M. Lester and C. Stivale (London: Continuum, 2003), 253–79, the concept of the *clinamen* (swerve) was invented as against the Atomists's claim about the motion of the particles supposed to take place always on a straight, linear line. According to Lucretius, the reason why the particles changed direction as they are moving on a straight line was because of the *clinamen*, which were included within the atoms and which had unpredictable free will of their own. This, without doubt, meant that both the animate and the inanimate were governed by an innate desire production.

FIGURE

Go and read Lacoue-Labarthe, in particular. In *Musica Ficta*,[1] after considering the impact of Wagner's music on a number of intellectuals of the times such as Baudelaire and Mallarmé but also Heidegger and Adorno, he discusses how a figure had been consistently made visible and hegemonic against an ideologically determined background. Michael Haneke's film *The White Ribbon* is a fine example of this situation. If Europe attempted to establish this with reference to Ancient Greece — nostalgia can easily be made ideological — what the West wants to establish today with reference to Islam (which will never be able to privatize the transcendental) is a figure simulation on the basis of a leader. If such a figure has become thoroughly representable today thanks to its media foregrounding at all levels, the only way to survive this situation is to ignore it, or rather to push it towards the realm of the unrepresentable. Please oh please, let's leave this figure outside the field of representation and see for ourselves how all this figuration has been a media-project — a project of stupification, clichéfication. See for yourselves, then, who would put on a white ribbon?

---

1 Philippe Lacoue-Labarthe, *Musica Ficta: Figures of Wagner*, trans. Felicia McCarren (Stanford: Stanford University Press, 1994).

HETERO-POWER-RAT

We would have always known this, but let's say it once again: if you are a leaf collector in this post-colonially constellated, fading out country, you are always second class, because what deserves attention here is to be an asparagus parrot of a tree highly esteemed by everyone. This is not too bad after all, in the slums but also in the posh neighborhoods of this town, for there is a hetero-power-rat who is always ready to verify his virility, and his food is always outside the home. You prepare snacks, he doesn't like them. You whistle but he will not obey. He drinks the raki of ressentiment. According to rumors, his remedy is to spare ice from his drink.

CAPITALISM, NEANDERTHALISM, AND THE DESPOT

Sometimes the one-in-power selects another-in-power who is directly opposed to the former in matters of signification so as to manipulate it towards a Hegelian synthesis as a result of which it will be enabled to occupy the foreground. Such a selection is usually made among the victims of *ressentiment* as in this way the victim of *ressentiment* will remain infinitely controllable by the one-in-power. Pushed into the foreground and having thus assumed a figure, the victim will always be kept in debt, and this economy of debt will be balanced in direct proportion to the capacity for producing a new synthesis at each step — that is, producing a capacity for being yoked more and more under each stage of a Hegelian *Aufhebung*. Debt should never be foreclosed. Yet there is something which the one-in-power may forget: the indebted may want to get rid of his debt and along come the shoe-boxes. This is the birth of Neanderthalism because the Neanderthal mindlessly interrupts the capital's circulation and its renewal through multiplication in his desire to store it in shoeboxes. On the other hand, the Neanderthal's system of signification has also gone out of control: despotic signification. The one-in-power apparently has not taken this into account: this Neanderthal who is picked up among the many due to his excess of *ressentiment* has now repositioned himself at the center of the signification system and started claiming that he is the source and reason of everything. While he is shouting out "Everything shall be mine," his disciples slaughter, rape, and ravish each other, affirming an identity that is not their own by shouting "Everything shall be his!" Then the one-in-power realizes in fear that he has invited the ghosts of pre-capitalism, the despot of feudalism, back onto the scene of history through his own will to power. Or, is it actually what he wanted, falsely imagining that he would be able keep the Neanderthal under his control at all costs? Yet the situation is clearly as follows: a system of *Aufhebung,* which works by overcoming the borders it is producing each moment by appropriating them the very next moment, is not functioning any more because of its byproduct, that is, Neanderthalism.

Looks like your end is near, despot! Not only because we want it to be so but because your signification system never captured us: you are the black sheep of capitalism. Not because we believe in capitalism, but because you gloriously short-circuit each other.

ORIENTALISM

Along the length of the road that stretches from Edward Said to Gayatri Spivak, the constellation of Orientalism has hit the ground in unforeseeable ways. The critique of the Western subject, which constituted its own subjectivity by dominating and othering the East, has transformed into the project of the construction of the Eastern subject who, having already been secularized by enforced modernism, is forced once again to privatize the transcendental within the absence of an opposition as such.[1] Yet here Spivak has committed a big mistake: Islam has never been a religion that let its transcendental be privatized and the project has thus ended up in the obliteration of the subject and its surrender to the transcendental. If this is one of the basic reasons why today the masses who desire repression, exploitation, and domination have been successfully created, another should be sought in the unprivatizable transcendental's capacity to be embodied in the figure of a profane despot in flesh and blood. Orientalism, which has turned into the preservation or the prolongation of the melancholia for the transcendental, is today a sinking ship.

---

1   Gayatri Spivak, "Terror: A Speech after 9-11," *Boundary 2* 31, no. 2 (2004): 81–111.

CONFESSION

If I have worked for the academy and rejected any administrative duty throughout all these years, it was all because to make their eyes blind in the sparkle of the academic and non-academic work that I have produced, which made my existence all the more irrelevant to them, which in turn made their existence equally irrelevant to me as we did not share a common language, mine always having been a minor one, to let them know I will never be counted as part of the "university = shopping mall" mentality that peaked especially after 2000s, because what has been real for me was to fabulate a line of flight with all my work outcast by the academy and to force them into admission by the institutions of stupidity, yet have you been able to do this Monsieur Xavier, yes, I have been, but no one is poisoned and died an unexpected death, still the pleasure I obtained from a toxic mode of being is incomparable to the daily inhibitions of nanofascism, the only way out for those feudal lords obtained from their hereditary recapitulations, which will end up at nought as the American middle-aged walk to the guillotine — 1970s porn.

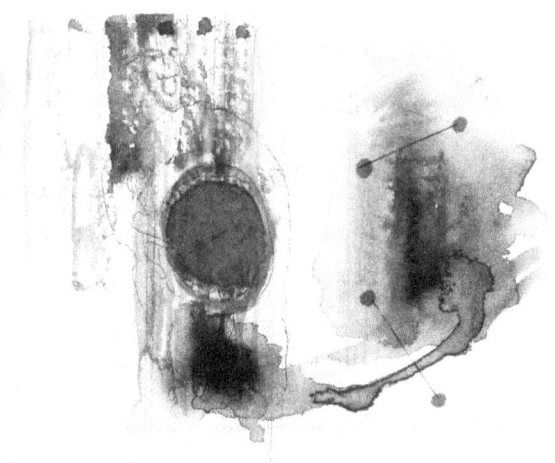

Fig. 1. "Last Vestiges of the Scream,"
watercolor, acrylic, pen, pencil, 15 × 20 cm, 2016.

BOREDOM

I am sick and tired of the ways in which heterosexual men and women think what they mix with what they vomit inside, when the high value that they ascribe to their sexual organs always falls under the estimated value with their *Realpolitik,* is literature, poetry, art, etc.

PARADOXICAL ELEMENT

In his "How Do We Recognize Structuralism?"[1] Deleuze draws attention to the essential element of structuralism: the arising of a new order which will function as the transcendental topology of the parts and their positions. In this order that we have inherited from Saussure, language will be a system comprised of differences without positive terms — that is, a structure where elements will determine each other only relationally. In this structure there is one special element traceable by transcendental topology, which Deleuze calls the paradoxical element: both lacking from the structure and in excess of it, the paradoxical element mobilizing the structure. This empty square, or "the occupant without a place" as he calls it in *The Logic of Sense*, can produce multiple forms without being localizable within the structure:

> The only place that cannot and must not be filled, were it even by a symbolic element. It must retain the perfection of its emptiness in order to be displaced in relation to itself, and in order to circulate throughout the elements and the variety of relations.[2]

According to speculative realists such as Benjamin Noys,[3] at the outset, Deleuze, by means of the creation of a negativity (a non-

---

[1] Gilles Deleuze, "How Do We Recognize Structuralism," in *Desert Islands and Other Texts 1953–1974*, ed. David Lapoujade, trans. Michael Taormina (New York: Semiotext(e), 2004), 170–92.
[2] Ibid., 189.
[3] Benjamin Noys, *The Persistence of the Negative: A Critique of Contemporary Continental Theory* (Edinburgh: Edinburgh University Press, 2010).

dialectical negativity) with this paradoxical element, invited a certain subject onto the scene of history, yet later rejecting this negativity, constructed his whole philosophy on the basis of pure affirmation. In my account, if this void, the occupant without a place, is to be taken as negativity, it can be taken thus only insofar as it is conceived neither in oppositional nor in conflictual terms; moreover, the fundamental issue at this juncture was what this subjectless subjectivity, awaited without being waited for, would do in the face of this non-dialectical negativity.

UN-MIMETIC

Do you recall Penthesilea? The Amazonian warrior in Heinrich von Kleist's play of the same title? A fractured representation of being a subject? Penthesilea is constructed neither as a full opponent of patriarchy nor as a passive subject crushed under unbridled masculinity. She has opened up a space for herself by shuttling between patriarchal and anti-patriarchal discourses and outraged all the epistemological and gender stabilities with her ironical language full of dualities and competing conflicts. It is as if Kleist had aimed at shaking the theory of representation of the Enlightenment down to its moralistic and ideological foundations in order to create a plane which cannot be constructed, where painting is impossible.

HEGEL-NANO-ORGANISM

To write a book, to make music, to read poems, to draw, to write an article, to give a talk, to whine, to moan — none of them is useful anymore — if there is no hope left, then let's set this negativity against pessimism, and think again. Perhaps we have always surrendered negativity to the hegemonic by means of the ways we have had of expressing ourselves. Perhaps due to a forced sense of positivity, due to our dread of affronting the Big Brother, we have expressed our demands trembling with fear, and perhaps sometimes compromising inch by inch with this monopoly of negativity, we have opened ourselves to narrow paths of survival … in conclusion, at the cost of repeating myself, we have to start seeing now that pessimism is of no use, and the real problem is to recapture negativity. Remember, it was you who voluntarily handed over the negativity which incessantly negates you by those sinister hands. They know nothing of Hegel but these days everything starts in such a moment of unknowing because there is a Hegel-Nano-Organism today and we must shed it from our cells.

NEANDERTHAL MANIFESTO

1. Neanderthals can never give birth to a figure when they are left to their own devices.

2. Neanderthals wander around in packs.

3. Neanderthals cannot produce desire; they become Neanderthal by interrupting desire production.

4. Neanderthals are not the society-against-state but the non-figural-against-society.

5. Neanderthals are not sexual; thus they do not go through becoming-sexual.

6. Neanderthals love despots and they follow the one whose voice utters first.

7. Neanderthals cannot produce goods but they like goods best.

8. Neanderthals lack memory therefore they always say, "No, we did not do that."

9. Neanderthals write poetry yet they always prefer impossible, murderous love affairs.

10. Neanderthals are without organs but they form immaculate bodies-with-organs when walking around in packs.

11. Neanderthals never learn how to read and write because they have a despot who constantly reads and writes them.

12. Neanderthals wage war against the figure although the figural is their arch-enemy.

13. Neanderthals like to take it from the front like a bolt out of the blue.

14. Neanderthals like the concrete, and eat roasted trees.

15. Neanderthals have a world but they cannot express it.

16. Neanderthals like an aesthetics which has not been theorized yet — they are in search of a Hegel but Odradek always runs away.

17. Neanderthals scream out loud whenever the figural comes into being, meaning to say, "It's mine, oh it's mine!"

18. Neanderthals don't like barter, their economy is homotopological, i.e., "there is nothing or no place which is not mine."

19. Neanderthals are *Homo Stupidus* according to Ernst Haeckel (1866).[1]

20. Neanderthals do not know what a cliché is; no, not even this.

---

1 F. Clark Howell, "The Evolutionary Significance of Variation and Varieties of 'Neanderthal' Man," *The Quarterly Review of Biology* 32, no. 4 (1957): 330–47.

TORN TO PIECES BUT STILL STANDING

Nano-fascism: the ultimate victory of the international league of fascism. We could at least deal with macro- and micro-fascism up to a point, but as nano-fascism is generated by political power's manipulation of schizophrenia which, once upon a time, we were accustomed to think of as emancipatory, things have become extremely difficult or even impossible to cope with. Schizo was emancipatory in the sense of denoting division, division into pieces, pieces not coming together to constitute a whole. By contrast, we still have the pieces, even more pieces today, but there is a voice now which, passing through each, dominates them: almost an *univocité* simulation. As Deleuze interpreted it, borrowing from Spinoza, *univocité* offered a non-ontological ontology by passing through each singularity and thus producing different expressions; it had no principle. In nano-fascism, this voice, passing through everyone, ends up producing the same expression in each, functioning as a transcendental ventriloquist. What happens to pieces in this case? In contrast to the previous situation — that is, instead of pieces flickering within a heterogenous structure — producing lines of flight in the present situation is made impossible. Everybody is torn to pieces but still standing and they shout out loud in unison: "No, we did not do it."

SUICIDE BOMBER

Neither philosophy nor arts nor music — everything boils down to the question of the human, all too human. Someone who has always hated being human gets caught up in the protocols of capitalism. We are living in a laboratory country and the name of the experiment is "How far can capitalism go?" How is it possible to construct an international exploitation system in the USA, Britain, France, and Germany with the results obtained from the laboratory, generally known as the East? We were happy to have molar structures — the comedy of humanity — until quite recently, because they made us aware of the fact that the human has never been very human. However, there is almost no hope left today: the negation — the human all too human — has infected even the smallest tissues of each and every body on a nano level. "So what?" asks everybody, everywhere. Specular structures everywhere encourage the desire to be a suicide bomber although it is only embodied within a molar structure, a Neanderthal but also a radical power, known as Islam, as of today. Here is my suggestion, comrades: against those fascist, anti-sharing, anti-life, anti-becoming, and at the same time anti-hauntological repressions, the only way to resist is to become a suicide bomber on an intellectual level — not in order to give up life but to force those who are forcing us to give up life to give up life. And this is the fundamental lack of Enlightenment today: Marquis de Sade/Büchner; critical perversion/somnambulist situationists.

MACRO/MICRO/NANO-FASCISM

Although it sounds as if it is a simple echo of the original German fascism, nano-fascism is a reappropriation of fascism by the Turkish Republic which has given birth to an islamo-capitalist-despotic-machine as a result of the redistribution of Western and Eastern capital into the monopoly of a despot. During the rise of German Nazism, it was obvious that the Führer came to power by monopolizing the libido, or the desiring-machine of each and every political subject in the nation. However, the way he managed this was largely dependent upon the extent to which he would be able to dominate the caesura between the *subject* of enunciation and the subject of *enunciation*. For example, in this phase, the Führer's ontological order established a transcendental subject on a macro level so far as the institutionalization of power was concerned. This power could be shared as long as one remained the subject of *enunciation*.

Micro-fascism, the continuation of macro-fascism into the post-war era, took the form of an "authoritarian personality," described so well by Adorno in a book of the same title.[1] In micro-facsicm, one did not need a Führer to dominate the caesura between *subject* of enunciation and the subject of *enunciation* because such a domination was already internalized and applied by the subject itself. This internal clock of fascism, namely micro-fascism, found expression also in Deleuze and Guattari's works as the distinction between the molar and molecular. In

---
1 Theodor W. Adorno Else Frenkel-Brunswik, Daniel Levinson, and Nevitt Sanford, *The Authoritarian Personality* (New York: Harper and Brothers, 1950).

this phase, capitalism's triumph lay in its ability to penetrate the molecular by way of freeing capital from a dependency on the economical, thereby creating pseudo-desiring-machines. It all meant an invitation to participate in the politics of ordinary daily life as long as one sacrificed the political, the preservation of which is crucial for the maintenance of micro/molecular distinction — the basis of the subject of enunciation.

The phase that I call nano-fascism is related to the forced appropriation of both macro and micro fascism by non-western countries such as Turkey. The tremendous amount of social, economic, and political repression in this country since the early 2000s has gone hand in hand with a violent monopolization of national and global capital: *Neanderthal Capitalism*. In this process, politicized Islam was the basic force, not allowing the privatization of the transcendental in contradistinction to Western constitutions based on the principle of laicism. As a result of this, even the distinction between *subject* of enunciation and the subject of *enunciation* is obliterated. Thus nano-fascism denotes neither a state where fascist repression is organized by institutions on a macro level, nor its internalization by the subject, rather, in nano-fascism one is born a nano-fascist. Being a product of Neanderthal Capitalism, the nano-fascist is the pre-individual non-singularity of post-Enlightenment whose world is dissolved into obedience without even knowing what obedience is.

ROMANTICISM

According to Lacoue-Labarthe and Nancy[2], it is Kantian philosophy which opens up the possibility of Romanticism. Due to an unforeseeable relationship established between philosophy and aesthetics in Kantian philosophy, a "passage" to Romanticism is made possible. Yet this relation is not something that can easily be put to work because where there should be a passage, a bridge, there is an abyss instead. Therefore this passage to Romanticism is actually a passage where nothing is allowed to pass. At the origin of this passage which allows nothing to pass, there is the subject emptied out by the Kantian transcendental. If what I call the "I" is unrepresentable except within the forms by means of which I make it representable to me, that is, if it is always bound to remain as a *phenomenon,* or, if it becomes knowable — outside the limits of the *noumenon* — only by means of representations of the "I" with reference to the transcendental, then what I call the "I" is an empty form. At one end of the abyss, there is this emptied form and, at the other, the transcendental imagination which will bestow on it infinite possibilities. Although a passage between the two is possible, since it will always be carrying a risk of failure, unavoidably it will end up in questions such as: "Is this the true form?" Having thus reached the status of an epistomologically unknowable, emptied-out form, the subject will be given the right of constructing itself on the levels of the social and the political only via its deeds of morality. Yet, this can be achieved only in the form of negation, in the form of

---

[2] Philippe Lacoue-Labarthe and Jean-Luc Nancy, *The Literary Absolute: The Theory of Literature in German Romanticism,* trans. Philip Barnard and Cheryl Lester (New York: SUNY Press, 1988).

a moral subjectivity which cannot produce knowledge of itself. It is as if the negativity it surrendered to the transcendental just in order to overcome the crisis of representation has opened up an infinite space of freedom before the moral subject, and thus it seems as if it will be able to constitute a consciousness — though it will not be able to produce an absolute knowledge — of itself. However, questions still remain, such as: Whose morality is this? Whose consciousness is this which the moral subject will constitute in the light of the formal question?

The Jena School[3] is the reversal of this abyss in aesthetic terms through the grounding of life on this absolutely impassable passage — or, in other words, by transforming life into a space of freedom comprised of absolutely artistic representations. Jena Romanticism would be perfectly Kantian if it did not include an element of "creation," if it did not see the world as the creation of a subject — in all its negativity, therefore, it means to turn one's back on the transcendental in matters of freedom. If the subject — not epistemologically, but morally — can create a consciousness and a world by its moral deeds, why would it still need to be formed by the transcendental? That which underlies this question is more horrifying than any possible way of answering it: just because it means the recognition of the fact that the world is made of the creations of a moral subject, made of its forms of representing the world to itself, opening up a route towards recapturing the negativity from the transcendental. The Jena School proposes a "political" which, by appropriating a negativity, becomes capable, though on micro levels, of questioning the authoritarian despotic, repressive regimes which

---

[3] Jena Romanticism or the Jena School is the first phase of Romanticism in German literature, represented by the work of a group centred in Jena from about 1798 to 1804. The movement is considered to have contributed to the development of German idealism in late modern philosophy. The group of Jena Romantics was led by the versatile writer Ludwig Tieck. Two members of the group, brothers August Wilhelm and Friedrich von Schlegel, laid down the theoretical basis for Romanticism in the circle's organ, the *Athenaeum*.

are established by the force of the transcendental. For example, Georg Büchner's *Lenz,* in this sense, is a novella where the politics of fixation maintained by concepts like citizen and citizenship is problematized. What happens if man leaves behind the politics of fixation exercised by authorities and sets out on the paths to schizophrenia? The *political*.

NOW

Is the future Queer? The future can never be queer because queer is fundamentally related to now, right up to this moment. Queer is now, that which is happening right now. To lay claim to now is to directly oppose heteronormativity. Since Aristotle, what we call now cannot be comprehended without presupposing concepts such as past and future, just as past and future cannot be constructed without presupposing a "now." As any intelligent person would know, here the real problem is that, although the past and the future cannot be constructed without "now," the latter is a concept which always flees from us. It is either too early or too late, or that which is always just about to happen. In contrast, the past is always in the past, and the future in the future.

Now there is a woman, and another woman, and the event is ciphered by masochism from the beginning. Roles are determined and everything works on the basis of a contract. Over and over again, this is a cipher with which the now is constructed on the basis of a contract. And later on the cipher stops being a cipher; it turns into something contained in the practice of those who think they are political, appropriating a *Realpolitik*. As the contract is obliterated, the now turns into past and future. Then we assume our roles, calculate our positions in politics.

Queer is the now of the past's unfulfilled promises of the future.

Fig. 2. "Last Vestiges of the Subject,"
watercolor, acrylic, pen, pencil, 15 × 20 cm, 2016.

THE SUBJECT

The real problem at this juncture is to comprehend the fact that the negative in Deleuze is not based on the production of a subject, a historical subject, and also that, since the produced negative is not conceptual (i.e., non-conceptual because it is not dialectical), it cannot call for a subject. Otherwise, to insist on the elaboration of a subject, an agent in conformity with traditional philosophy hidden in Deleuzian philosophy, is to force the negative in Deleuze to a position on a Hegelian/Marxist axis.

SOMNAMBULIST SITUATIONISTS

The main inspiration behind *I Want to be a Suicide Bomber*[1] was the approaching moment of delirium to be reached as a result of the capsule of capitalism that the West forced its in-dividuals[2] to swallow. My intention was to make visible this moment of delirium by quotations I took from 100 different books, songs, films, and photographs. What I wanted to underline was that the seeds of such a moment of delirium were already incubating in each individual in the West and the explosion to come was only a matter of time. The West had had good breaks so that it had been successful in avoiding such a moment of explosion as of then, and the explosions were taking place only in the East, until recently. However, as we have all borne witness, ISIS arose in the course of time and a good number of its participants came from the West. The seeds of being a suicide bomber were coming to fruition imminently also in the West.

In other words, no matter whether you desired it or not, to be a suicide bomber was an act which capitalism and a religion which does not allow its transcendental to be privatized were forcing its followers into. Even if you did not say, "I Want to be a Suicide Bomber," you were bound to be one. Now the situation has altered slowly as the West — primarily France and the US — has commenced applying the results it obtained from its laboratory called Turkey on its own citizens. Against Trump,

---

1   Sherif Xenoph Ibn el Somnambulist Situationists Constantinople, *I Want to Be a Suicide Bomber* (San Francisco: Little Black Cart Books, 2013).
2   "In-dividual" and "-dividual" are used to express indivisibility and divisibility respectively: an infinite divisibility against a finite one.

who is today the world's bloodiest suicide bomber, together with Erdogan and Putin, to be followed by Le Pen, there will arise the somnambulist situationists! *Vive la résistance!*

WISH

I don't like religions, actually I hate them. Enthroning ignorance, they reject enlightenment though not in the fashion of a Marquis de Sade or Adorno and Horkheimer. They have the right to confiscate everything; they like bombs; they love to be number one wherever immorality, theft, and murder is concerned. They even wish for a world without a tape where they will always win without a race. As they do with anything else, they manipulate fasting in order to usurp the rights of others as appetizers on dinner tables. My God, if you exist, please turn them into booze and drink them, please prove that you do not exist so that the roasted chick peas return and those Neanderthal, pre-individual non-singularities don't blossom any more.

REPRESENTATION

Just walk down Lüleci Hendek Street and right after you pass Depo Gallery on the left, first turn right and then left, and there you are: Tophane Park in Istanbul. For more than a year the Neanderthals were renovating the park and its environment and, as you would remember, they re-cemented the pavements surrounding the park in such a way that the trees were almost smothered to death. Now at the entrance of the park they have erected a disaster of representation. It is entitled *Nusrat Torpedo Boat* and it's dedicated to the captain of the boat Lieutenant Ismail Bey of Tophane. Obviously, representation in art has a special sense in their minds. Art has to represent everything as in a one-to-one relationship, and the duty of the artist is to re-enact — to animate — things in an exact correspondence with reality. I especially picked up the term "to animate" because each work of art has a tendency to bring back to life that which is dead or that which does not exist any more — to breathe life into that which is not alive any more. Yet what endows the work of art with an aesthetic value lies in an ability to saturate the work with a capacity to short-circuit this process of animation; the more spectres of non-resemblance visit the work, the closer it gets to an aesthetic value. Representation in the arts, in contrast to what happens in an ethnographic museum, is what never comes back to life completely. Now, if we look at the torpedo boat from this perspective, we can understand why we get so very scared. The spectre has gained full materiality: the torpedos are floating in the represented sea, and the sea is undulating in frozen forms of pure resemblance; everything has been almost completely and substantially animated or massively substantialized to transform the scene of representation into an ideologically manipulated scene of hallucination. This is how animation is murdered or still-born due to a privileging of representation over spectralization. In contrast, the spectres are spectres insofar as they complicate the borders of visibility; and, in being so, they trigger an artistic pleasure rather than fear. Dear Neanderthals, art is not your school of theology; you cannot blame the rage you have for a religion which does not allow you to privatize the transcendental on your practice of animating everything absolutely, and thereby transforming things into ghouls of representation.

WHEN WILL THEY COME TO AN END?

1. When everyone except them starts speaking a bird language;

2. When they all become flower pots on window sills of different heights;

3. When they stop dreaming of getting laid by their despot;

4. When they all fall in love with the tortoise in Zeno's paradox;

5. When they all buy black market tickets for an Aphex Twin gig;

6. When they all learn that Allah is a machine for loving schizophrenia;

7. When they all realize that to learn by heart the prayers from Koran is not the same as aesthetics;

8. When they all give up the idea of going back home;

9. When everyone except them becomes an Andalusian Dog;

10. When they all become annoyed for not walking on their heads.

IN MEMORIAM ULUS BAKER[1]

Whenever the name of Ulus Baker is mentioned with regard to Deleuze studies in Turkey, we are faced with some vexing problems about his reception. The first of these is that Ulus was the type of a person who would always stand against iconization or canonization. Without doubt, it was unavoidable that around his name would gather a hippie cult — just as in the case of Brian Massumi — when there were too many people attached to him, pushing him into a position of a guru. Yet Ulus never became a guru and, therefore, he never became a Žižek-esque clown of thought. The second, considering especially the possibilities of becoming of the body in Deleuzian thought, is that Ulus's way of being resembled the ways in which the progression of psychoanalysis — as is well-explained by Abraham and Torok[2] — would be possible only by going bankrupt. If the body was a god-given form and what we had to do in order to get rid of this organization of body *à la* Artaud was to shake metaphysics, how was one supposed make a body without a body? Seen from this perspective, it is impossible not to be reminded of this chapter from Deleuze and Guattari's *A Thousand Plateaus*[3]: "How Do

---

[1] Ulus Baker (1960–2007) was an intellectual figure who introduced Deleuzian philosophy to Turkish academia and influenced a generation of young people with his extensive number of publications on sociology, politics, and philosophy.

[2] See Nicholas Abraham and Maria Török, *The Shell and the Kernel: Renewals of Psychoanalysis, Volume 1*, trans. Nicholas T. Rand (Chicago: The University of Chicago Press, 1994), and *The Wolfman's Magic Word: A Cryptonomy*, trans. Nicholas T. Rand (Minneapolis: University of Minnesota Press, 1986).

[3] Gilles Deleuze and Félix Guattari, *A Thousand Plateaus: Capitalism and Schizophrenia*, trans. Brian Massumi (Minneapolis: University of Minnesota Press, 1987).

You Make Yourself A Body Without Organs?" There are dangers and there are choices: it all wavers between being lifeless and not preferring life. Not everyone can be so brave so as to decide to return to pre-individual singularities. Actually Ulus did not achieve this either, and herein lies the mythology. What we are left with today are his works of genius; shining, bright; instead of nostalgic and narcissus-like repetitions, we must go on, GO ON!

THE THING

When we look at the concept of citizenship in Ancient Greece, we come across a group of people who do not know either the sedentary life or agriculture; being basically nomadic, they stand against everything that is settled. As the main reason behind the collapse of each civilization until 6 BCE lies the disastrous effect of nomadic invasions. At the origin of what we know as cities today shines the Greek "polis" which grants ultimately selective rights of citizenship to its inhabitants. For example, according to Aristotle, slaves in Ancient Greek cities should be considered as "things" because they don't have souls (*psukhē*). Until Plato, *psukhē* is imagined as something which can return, revisiting the living at any time even after the death of the body. The clarity and precision of thought starts only when the return of the *psukhē* is prohibited by Plato. Now, if we consider not only the Syrian immigrants but also the ones who, in broader terms, appropriated the nomadic way of life as their raison d'être, we can start to see that the real problem arises not fundamentally from racism but also from the fear of risking our safe lives based on the prohibition of the return of the uncanny. One thing to be realized here is how ready we are to forget, to lose our concept of citizenship at the cost of getting rid of our sedentary, settled lives? What if all things — i.e., all of us are things under Neanderthal Capitalism — decide to return? What happens if we all return?

PESSIMISM

each day we are bombarded by the layers of the episteme such as obama said this and that and there will be no gas pipelines from russia no it was only fifteen minutes before the djinns would possess him because organizations can be divided into five types etc. etc. in other words take each branch and plot each and make your own plots and get scared get frightened of everything to draw your own borders but fail to create your own lines of flight as you give some incidents as gifts to those who leave you breathless victimizing yourself at the same time but no I am not talking about nihilism neither saying right sit back and relax didn't they murder people on the mountains I mean nazis therefore there is only one distinction that is the good and the bad and beyond the good and the bad no still I am not talking about pessimism yet if such is the situation if this is the situation i.e. the situation of everyone against everyone that is zero analysis I am the zero then and I wait and wait without waiting more or less

"when all the hope is gone there is no reason for pessimism"[1]

---

[1] Aki Kaurismäki, quoted in Simon Hattenstone, "Seven Rounds with Aki Kaurismäki," *The Guardian,* April 4, 2012, https://www.theguardian.com/film/2012/apr/04/aki-kaurismaki-le-havre-interview.

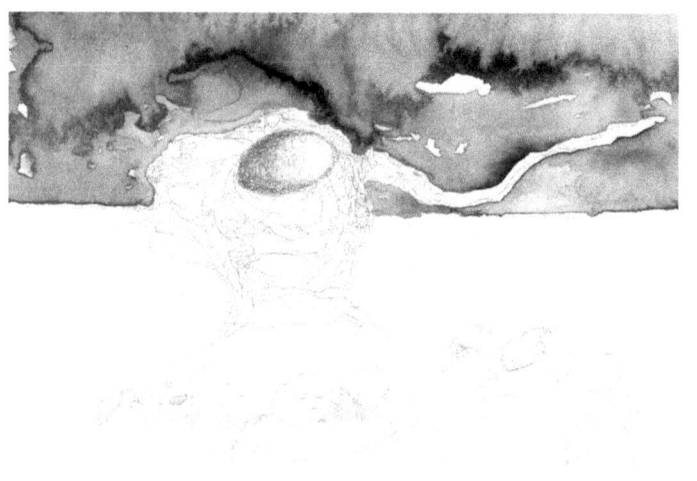

Fig. 3. "Last Vestiges of Becoming-Child," watercolor, acrylic, pen, pencil, 15 × 20 cm, 2016.

SCHIZO-INCEST

I had suggested, in my book, *Desonance,* that the real problem with the paradoxical element in Deleuze's *The Logic of Sense* (1969) lay not in its desire to call a subject into being but in the question of localizability[1]. At that time, rather than seeing it as a problem of negativity, I saw this as a problem — in contrast to a Lacan-influenced approach which revolved around the unlocalizability of this element, the occupant without a place — emanating from the paradoxical element's localizability as a result of a certain passage from nothingness into being. Then, in my *Atopological Trilogy,*[2] claiming that this is a problem of atopology rather than topology, I shifted the discussion from an unsolicited subject to something which was not in the least related to the question of the subject: schizo-incest.

---

1 Zafer Aracagök, *Desonance: Desonating (with) Deleuze* (Saarbrücken: VDM Verlag, 2009).
2 Zafer Aracagök, *Atopological Trilogy: Deleuze and Guattari* (Brooklyn: punctum books, 2015).

APPLICATION

Deleuze and Guattari started producing their philosophical works during early phases of neo-liberalist ideology; one of the main intentions of *Anti-Oedipus,* which can also be read as a critique of the capitalist axiomatic, was to ward off ontology from thought, something which has traditionally attached to philosophy on every occasion. Despite all their efforts, if such a warding off has been transformed into a coagulation of "form" today — the golden age of neo-liberalism — then the reason for failure should be sought in how we understand the relationship between the plane of consistency and the plane of organization. In other words, the biggest of all the failures is the one which has turned philosophy, but particularly the philosophy of Deleuze and Guattari, into a matter of applicability. Can we please save our readings from the yoke of the "mimetic"?

PLATO, MIMESIS, COUP D'ÉTAT

In the tenth chapter of Plato's *Republic*, there is a discussion about mimesis. For example, a carpenter has produced a chair according to an idea of a chair but when you sit on it you realize that there is something wrong with the chair. In this case, you take the chair to the carpenter, and tell him your complaints, and the carpenter reworks the chair to get it closer to its ideal form, that is, to produce a perfect resemblance between the chair and its ideal form. What is important here is to create a one-to-one mimetic equivalence between the model and the copy. Things get complicated when we consider the artist who makes a painting of the chair, because now we are in a situation where we cannot use and tell whether the copied chair is useful or not. According to the argument, since artistic representation does not allow us to test the usefulness of the produced copy, and since it tells us lies, the arts should be expelled from the *Republic*. Now, if we look at the logic of the *coup d'état* from this angle, has this incident put forward something which cannot be verified on the basis of a perfect correspondence between the thing and its idea, the failure of which cannot be reported to the interested authorities, such as a carpenter? Or rather, do we overlook the proliferation of various possible meanings since we already have the tendency of overriding artistic representation? Without doubt, we need a bit of the notion of *quod libet* so as to save these choices from the straightjacket of the useful. It is only thus we can prefer not to prefer, like Bartleby. A situation where non-representability is preferred. Meta-democracy?

THE FIGURE

We are living in such a period of suffocation that the lines get caught up in the contours, and the political of the figural finds embodiment only in the *Gestalt* of *Realpolitik* where we imagine two dots appearing on the horizon and no sooner have they appeared then the despot gets hold of them, draws out a face from them, and places himself at the top of all the signifiying chains, turning it into a poison that is the poison of belonging they call democracy, the black milk of which we drink everyday.[1]

Still the line sometimes breaks away, wandering upside down with Lenz in the forests falling into heart-breakings and then shaking off everything upsurging to the surface. Obviously it will not let them inscribe those words on its skin, as there are lines of flight from the colony — insofar as one is horizonless *à la* Blanchot.

---

[1] Paul Celan, "Fugue of Death," in *Selected Poems,* trans. Michael Hamburger and Christopher Middleton (Harmondsworth: Penguin Books, 1972), 33–34.

AUFHEBUNG IN REVERSE

You can call it just another conspiracy theory, but I shall insist on claiming that the neo-liberalist governments all around the world since the 1990s, pushing the concept of democracy towards its outside, have successfully constituted a territory of "extra-democracy"; and reaching their citizens from the territory of this outside — the metaphysics of fraudery — they govern and manipulate elections. Now this being of the outside not only manipulates each vote via metaphysics, but it has also thoroughly penetrated the election systems. Wherever we are in the world today — makes no difference if you are in the UK, Turkey, the US, Poland, Egypt, or Russia, etc. — we complain about the elections, the results of which we could not predict, and blame it all on the disappearance of the Left. Without doubt, the Left has been on the wane since the '70s yet obviously the discourse which propounds the idea that "people have completely lost their hope and they want to try something new and therefore they vote for the fascists" is being forced and imposed upon the masses by the invisible hands of this metaphysics of fraudery. All this hides but one truth: that although each and every administrative system of this kind foists off on the people that it works on the principle of a Platonic concept of democracy, these sysems, in a relationship with the territory of extra-democracy, — that is, with the outside of the concept of democracy — corrupt themselves by means of a negativity, meticulously preserved as conflict with the aid of an *Aufhebung* in reverse. In this era, history does not repeat itself but is forced to repeat itself.

THE KING-FISH

The idea that one has to continue to work and produce no matter how dire the situation applies only to those places where at least the minimum requirements of democracy are met. Work is not only produced but it emanates from a social contract: if such a contract by means of which the work is put into circulation is abrogated, life runs the risk of turning into a pointless practice. Of course, there are differences between different types of practices.

As rumor has it, Turkey will become a prosperous country when it is discovered why the king-fish swim against the current right up to the rivers' sources and, once there, turn around in circles aimlessly for days on end.

It is high time to start research on the Origins of Stupidity in Turkey.

WHITE NOISE

When McLuhan argued that "the medium is the message," he was satisfied with claiming that the form in which the message was molded was actually the message itself. Yet this medium, if we consider it from a Deleuze-Guattarian point of view, is a flow which assumes a form only when its flow is interrupted. That you have a radio or a TV doesn't necessarily mean that you are supposed to perceive a message which has assumed a form. You can listen to or look at the "white noise" without being tuned to a certain frequency on your radio or TV for days on end. To perceive is also an ideological construction as well as that which forces you to perceive.

Fig. 4. "Last Vestiges of Affirmation," watercolor, acrylic, pen, pencil, 15 × 20 cm, 2016.

MAPS AND COORDINATES

In one of the short stories[1] by Borges, there is a talk about a map which, thousands of years ago, covered the whole Empire. In time, the art of cartography and cartographers lost their prominence and the remnants of maps of such huge scale, scattered around in deserts, were left to disuse. According to Baudrillard, as we know, today there's nothing left to us from the times when an exact one-to-one relationship between reality and its representation could be established, not even a representable reality, and hence we have delved into the age of simulation: in other words, into the world of images which do not correspond to a reality. Today, the situation is utterly modified: international Neanderthal capitalism and colonialism have now reconstructed that lost reality; yet the latter, should you not know how to see or have lost your powers of resistance, is a big lie. Today, we have regained the map as well as "the reality" but, although the directions are offered as indeterminable, the map is completely topological and your coordinates are absolutely determinable, making you always already surrendered to the police.

---

1 Jorge Luis Borges, "On Exactitude in Science," in *Collected Fictions,* trans. Andrew Hurley (London: Penguin Books, 1999), 325.

APORIA

The paranoiac machine feeds on the despot's desire to attach all the signifying chains to himself; it is expected that each link in the chain would vibrate with corrosion and thus get into resonance with one another. Each bit of corrosion added to the field of resonance would be devoured with greed so that the resonance coefficient obtained from the links will hit the heights. This is how a shield comes into being, yet it is mostly overlooked that the shield is aporetic. Oh, *aporia,* what will you do in the midst of this Neanderthal capitalism?

THE ARTWORK

Each artwork hopelessly dreams of the day it will have an immediate impact on the spectator. The day will come when there will be no unsurpassed hill, river, excitement, joy, scream, love — whatever — left between the artwork and its spectator, and the two, leaving behind all the protocols of pornography, will be completely and infinitely intertwined with one another. At the same time, the realization of such a moment will also bring with it the bitter end of art because at such a moment, not only will the Kantian determinations of time and space disappear, leaving no need for art, but also the path from the *in-dividual* (which makes man an indivisible unity) to *-dividual* (that is, the divisible) will be opened where the nature/human dichotomy will dissolve, dissolving man in turn into a psychasthenic universe. In such a moment, when infinity and man will embrace each other mutually, there will be no occurrence of expressions such as "Where are you? I don't know. What time is it? I don't know"; the cosmic dust cloud made of human grains will allow no synthetic structure to come into being, and most probably no one will be able to claim any more a theory of "abiogenesis" — "But if (& oh what a big if) we could conceive in some warm little pond with all sorts of ammonia & phosphoric salts, — light, heat, electricity, &c present, that a protein compound was chemically formed, ready to undergo still more complex changes ..."[1]

---

[1] Charles Darwin, "Letter to Joseph Dalton Hooker" (February 1, 1871), *Darwin Correspondence Project,* https://www.darwinproject.ac.uk/letter/DCP-LETT-7471.xml.

NEGATION OF NEGATION VS. AFFIRMATION

In *Difference and Repetition*,[1] particularly in sections written on negativity, Deleuze, discussing the distinction between "being and non-being" and "being and *non*-being," rejects the consideration of the latter under the aegis of Hegelian dialectics. He is talking about Plato's *The Sophist* and according to him at this stage it is not yet possible to determine thought on the basis of dialectics. The non-being does not mean negativity—it is the problematic.[2] The negative is always secondary with regard to the positive, and it works always as the shadow (*Nachfolge*) of the real, that is, the positive. Rather than being obtained as a result of a double negation as in a Hegelian move, the primacy of the positive or affirmation is due to Nietzsche's philosophy of Eternal Return (*die ewige Wiederkehr*). Deleuze's elaborations on the Eternal Return come from Nietzsche's Zarathustra and accordingly the Eternal Return is posited as that which never brings back that which is not positive, that which does not affirm itself, and it is in this way the return of the non-affirmative is obstructed. With this move, the Eternal Return puts forward a new approach to the positive obtained by the negation of the negative: the negated or that which has to be negated should be rejected because the negative which follows from the primacy of the positive as its shadow cannot pass the test of the Eternal Return. Why can't it pass? All because the negative is the reduction

---

1 Gilles Deleuze, *Difference and Repetition*, trans. Paul Patton (London and New York: Continuum, 2001).
2 Ibid., 64.

of all the differences which builds up the Eternal Return down to its identity; subsuming difference under opposition (that is, A ≠ B), it yields to identity and it achieves this by means of representation. In contrast, the eternal formlessness of the Eternal Return cannot allow such identity and representation. To represent is the same as forcing that which is made of differences into the straitjacket of the conceptual. The concept cannot represent the difference in its being always different from itself, and in this respect the Platonic idea is above the concept because it has not yet developed the concept of an object and therefore it has not yet surrendered the world to the protocols of representation: it is only mentioned as a function of those things which cannot be represented in the objects in the world. In short, the idea has not yet related difference to the concept's method of reducing difference to identity. At such a juncture, where the precursor of a non-conceptual affirmation occupies the horizon, it can be seen why Deleuze rejects negation: negation as the shadow of affirmation reduces a formless structure down to a conceptual form, and thus maintains an identity via oppositions.[3]

We should immediately stress that there is a difference between Platonic "*non*-being" and Hegelian "non-being" because in Plato there is no qualitative difference between "being" and "*non*-being" and the positive is not maintained by a double negation: the positive is already claimed as primary as a result of the affirmation of all the differences. This is why "*non*-being" is not the being of the negative but of the problematic (problems and questions). It is only in Hegelian dialectics that difference is reduced to identity as a result of setting "being" and "non-being" into an opposition, and the problem is resolved by a dialectics, that is, by the force of the negation of the negation and the ensuing synthesis.

Dialectics is led astray by exchanging the vacillation between the difference and the differential with the negative; and it

---

3   Ibid., 54–59.

reaches its peak in Hegel. Instead of being defined by "*non*-being," which means the "being" of problems and questions, the dialectics is now defined by non-being which means the "being" of the negative. An origin maintained by a complimentary relationship between the positive and the affirmative is now replaced by that which is produced by the negative; and, therefore, it is maintained by the negation of the negation, passing itself off as the origin of affirmation.

PROJECT

After the death of Deleuze and then Derrida, French philosophy has also taken its share from global conservatism. For example, Badiou's philosophy, although it has its own value, introduced an ontology, a mathematical one, into Deleuzian philosophy which Deleuze himself carefully and intentionally kept away from his thought. Badiou's project was to rehabilitate Deleuze and Guattari's interpretation of Marx so as to make it function programmatically.

However, one of the basic concerns of Deleuze-Guattarian philosophy is to demonstrate how thought works by failing to work, by stammering, just like life itself which normally flows by failing to flow. To introduce Hegel into thought means to reconstruct that grand narrative at the cost of falling into the ditch of metaphysics. At the root of such advances lies, without doubt, the intention to erase the radicality of the philosophy of both Derrida and Deleuze by dissolving it into academic arrogance. For example, to introduce Hegel into Derrida means to affirm the rejection of metaphysics in absolute and oppositional terms, which Derrida himself never did. You cannot reach anywhere with Derridaean philosophy and the main reason behind this is the recognition of metaphysics as a trace that constructs and deconstructs thought both by its presence and absence. The rise of philosophers such as Badiou, Laruelle, and Malabou after the death of Deleuze and Derrida is wholly of a piece with a certain political project. After the radical critique of Structuralism, the rupture of thought brought about by a way of thinking that claimed it is the nature of thought to think what it cannot think or by the inclusion of the unthought within thought in a plane of immanence, not only disturbed the integrity of philosophy, but it also put at stake the darling of philosophy: the subject. For all these reasons, the above mentioned philosophers who came after Deleuze and Derrida are part of a project for rebuilding the *in-dividual* against *-dividual*.

CASTRATORS OF DESIRE

It's the mid-1970s and I am in Izmir, Turkey. As part of the weekly fun-rituals for kids, mom is taking us to Kemeraltı: döner kebab, ice-cream puddings, rice puddings, caramel puddings, and moreover Vimpi (predecessor of the hamburger, made of meatballs, egg and cheese). There is POP, a music magazine in German which I buy every month with my savings because the glam kings THE SWEET are my favorite band, and each issue features their posters and pics; I order platform shoes from different dealers, BAY CITY ROLLERS-type checkered trousers, and fall in love with the Sean Connery of ZARDOZ and the Jane Fonda of BARBARELLA. There are some streets around the Namazgah exit of Kemeraltı and whenever we go there to shop for fabrics, buttons, or threads I am scared to death as there are some utterly ugly, stumpy shop owners with short-cropped moustaches whom I usually don't see in daily life. Their breath smells of mosque, berlingots, sherbet, and ashure and I am disgusted with their desiring gaze directed to my mom as well as to us and I want to run away from their shops as soon as I can. Now, as the years have passed, their lust has grown into a monument and hijacked our desire.

MICHAEL KOHLHAAS

I suggest that Heinrich von Kleist's novella *Michael Kohlhaas*[1] should be considered together with the crisis of representation opened by Kantian philosophy. At the beginning of the story, Kohlhaas is an honest, pious, merciful, charitable horse dealer and a good "citizen" who lives in harmony with his family and environment. One day as he is en route to a horse market nearby in Saxony to sell his horses, he is stopped by the guards of the landowner who ask him for his documents of permission to pass through the lands of their lord. Up until this time, Kohlhaas has passed seventeen times through these lands without documents and in face of such a request he has to leave two of his horses as hostage. That this will be an impassible passage where nothing is allowed to pass will be clearer to Kohlhaas when he later on learns from the related civil office that he does not actually need to possess such documents for his journey, and especially when on his way back from the market he finds out his horses have been misused and worn out due to heavy work and lack of food. Although he applies to the court many times for his damages to be recompensed by the landlord, his cases are rejected one by one by the Saxon bureaucratic state machine. And in the face of the lawlessness of the law, Kohlhaas starts a pure war against the class which counts as the earthly representative of the transcendental. The philosophical framework of the evolution he will go through all throughout the novella is limited by the extent to which his consciousness, that is, the consciousness of the moral subject determined by the transcendental, will allow him. Al-

---

1   Heinrich von Kleist, *Michael Kohlhaas,* trans. Martin Greenberg (Brooklyn: Melville House, 2005).

though the law has been established by a Rousseauesque social contract based on the absolutization of the transcendental, what assumes visibility in Kohlhaas' struggle is the following fundamental question: Whose transcendental is this?

The death of his wife, and the villages and towns he devastates with his civil army do not add to his victory over the noble Junker von Tronka, the violator of the law, who always slips away from his hands, and all this leads Kohlhaas to reject the necessity to obey the rule of the transcendental. Consequently, leaving behind the concept of "good citizenship" dictated to him by the state and religion, and fighting against the state machine which fails to be impartial, failing to return his rights to him, Kohlhaas drifts from one plunder to another, violates the borders of negativity and thus turning himself into a nomad-machine. This is actually a revolt against the power of the transcendental fixing, stabilizing, or immobilizing its obedients as "citizens." Setting himself free from the yoke of a necessity whereby one is obliged to represent oneself to oneself via the sovereignty of the transcendental, there is an infinite space of freedom opened up before Kohlhaas. It is this opening which decrees the passage impassable because from this moment on there is no need left for a passage. It is the disappearance of such a need which returns negativity to Kohlhaas. Kant's moral subject now discovers not immorality but extra-morality by means of which they will turn upside down all the rules of morality and the transcendental according to their own will-to-power just as it will be expressed in Nietzsche's philosophy at the end of the nineteenth century. Moreover, from now on, Kohlhaas will build his life with the actuality of a here and now, reaching towards a realm beyond mimesis.

Towards the end of the novella, we observe how this space of freedom opened before Kohlhaas is retrieved, taken back, measure by measure, from him by fraudery. What he has always claimed will eventually be returned to the horse-dealer, yet it will not save him from execution due to his violation of the laws of the transcendental. In the face of such an approaching disaster, Heinrich von Kleist resorts to calling metaphysics to his aid. In a capsule hanging on a chain around his neck, Kohlhaas keeps a secret letter he received from a gypsy fortune teller that reveals the fate of a certain member of the nobility, the Saxon Elector, one of the members of the gang who has obstructed Kohlhaas's struggle for justice. Right before the moment the executioner lets fall the hatchet on his neck, Kohlhaas opens up the capsule and swallows the secret letter. As a result, no matter how the future may have contained a moment of hope, the future of this very hope is swallowed and the passage is claimed as impassable for the representatives of the transcendental as well.

The abyss opened up in philosophy by Kant will in future be synthesized by Hegel, and master-slave dialectics will be claimed as universal by submitting the construction of a subject into the hands of an ideology of historical progress in direct proportion to the unfolding of Absolute Spirit. Kleist wrote that he finds it "incomprehensible how a human being can live without a plan for his life [*Lebensplan*],"[2] yet his lifetime of thirty-four years of drifting from one place to another goes a long way to showing that life doesn't accept any *Lebensplan*, and his suicide lays bare the fact that we can regain freedom with a conceptless negativity if we really will it.

---

2 Heinrich von Kleist, *The Marquise of O— and Other Stories,* ed. and trans. David Luke and Nigel Reeves (New York: Penguin Books, 1978), 7.

NEANDERTHAL RATIONALITY

On October 9, 2016, a year ago, my exhibition of watercolors, *Taking from Behind,* opened and the next day we woke to another suicide bombing, an outrageous mass murder at Ankara Train Station. The title of the show, without doubt, had nothing to do with this treacherous act of murder. *Taking from Behind* was rather a war declared against the dispositives of Neanderthal rationality interrupting the flow of thought, against the hegemonic discourses transforming the figural into the figurative: those who are forced to immortal sleep, please know that we are waiting for you — Lady Lazarus.

LITERATURE

> To write is not to recount one's memories and voyages, one's loves and griefs, one's dreams and phantasms. It is the same thing to sin through an excess of reality as through an excess of the imagination. In both cases it is the eternal daddy-mommy, an Oedipal structure that is projected onto the real or introjected into the imaginary. In this infantile conception of literature, what we seek at the end of the voyage, or at the heart of a dream, is a father.[1]

It's understandable that some people were disturbed when Bob Dylan was offered the Nobel Prize for Literature. Nevertheless I'd like to remind them Bob Dylan is *Highway 61 Revisited*, *Blonde on Blonde*, *Blood on the Tracks*, and *Desire*, and and and … long before the rubbish pop inaugurated by The Beatles in the 1960s, it was also he who radically changed musical forms under the influence of the Beat Generation, dreamt of an America without the Vietnam War, mediated the reality of that concrete situation in "All Along the Watchtower," and, finally, it was him and only him who sang "Something is happening, but you don't know what it is, do you, Mr Jones?" Beatniks were kids without a father. What did those kids without a father achieve? Some of them hit the road without a destination in mind, much in the spirit of the early German Romantics, and talked about the virtues of getting lost, shedding the subject positions tailored for them by mass culture, while some of them, removing the tradition of telling a story from what is known as the novel,

---

[1] Gilles Deleuze, "Literature and Life," trans. Daniel W. Smith, *Critical Inquiry* 23, no. 2 (1997): 225–30.

uprooted the balanced, distanced relation between subject and object — *The Naked Lunch* — thereby leading literature to the ways in which schizo-incest informed all acts of writing.

In a chapter called "The Connectors" in their Kafka book,[2] Deleuze and Guattari distinguish in Kafka's work a class of women who are "part sister, part maid, part whore," who are basically "anti-conjugal, anti-familial"[3] and constitute a line of flight from Oedipal familial ties on the basis of "freedom of movement, freedom of statement, freedom of desire."[4] The group of "sister-maid-whore"[5] produces a desire on the basis of masochism so that it not only undoes limitations or rigid subject positions brought about by Oedipal ties but it also renders possible the other two aspects of freedom. In the first place, in contrast to neurotic Oedipal incest which occurs with the mother, schizo-incest takes place with the sister and is an incest of deterritorialization. Belonging to a universal paranoid machine, Oedipal incest has no liberative moment because it falls prey to what has prohibited it — that is, the paranoiac transcendental law and therefore continuously reterritorializes whatever it has given freedom. Yet, what is most striking in their theorization is the fact that while Oedipal incest is connected to images, schizo-incest is connected to sound with a maximum of connections, operating through a continuous deterritorialization

---

2 Gilles Deleuze and Félix Guattari, *Kafka: Toward a Minor Literature,* trans. Dana Polan (Minneapolis: University of Minnesota Press, 1986).
3 Ibid., 64.
4 Ibid., 65.
5 Ibid., 66: "This combined formula, which has value only as an ensemble, is that of schizo-incest. Psychoanalysis, because it understands nothing, has always confused two sorts of incest: the sister is presented as a substitute for the mother, the maid as a derivative of the mother, the whore as a reaction-formation. The group of 'sister-maid-whore' will be interpreted as a kind of masochistic detour but, since psychoanalysis also doesn't understand anything about masochism, we don't have to worry much about it either."

towards the unformed, liberating each familial or Oedipal tie from predetermined rules based on a fixed image of thought.[6]

During the mid-2010s, while I was staying in a hotel in Paris, the receptionist from Montenegro, excited to hear that I was from Istanbul, asked me whether I knew a certain Turkish writer, Orhan Pamuk, whose books she read feverishly. I told her that I'd never heard this name before and I didn't know a man of literature with this name. It wouldn't make any difference if Bob Dylan was not offered a Nobel Prize; as Leonard Cohen put it: "It is like giving a prize to Mount Everest for being the highest mountain." Yet, Yaşar Kemal!

---

6   Ibid., 67: "Schizo-incest corresponds, in contrast, to the immanent schizo-law and forms a line of escape instead of a circular reproduction, a progression instead of a transgression [...]. Oedipal incest is connected to photos, to portraits, to childhood memories, a false childhood that never existed but that catches desire in the trap of representation, cuts it off from all connections, fixes it onto the mother to render it all the more puerile or spoiled [...]. Schizo-incest, in contrast, is connected to sound, to the manner in which sound takes flight and in which memory-less childhood blocks introduce themselves in full vitality into the present to activate it, to precipitate it, to multiply its connections. Schizo-incest with a maximum of connection, a polyvocal extension, that uses that uses as an intermediary maids and whores and the place that they occupy in the social series — in opposition to neurotic incest, defined by its suppression of connection, its single signifier, its holding of everything within the limits of the family, its neutralization of any sort of social or political field."

THE DREAM

Starting every day waking up from uncanny dreams. This time we are in Çeşme. We are located at one end of the Boyalik bay; and when I turn my eyes to the opposite end I see the horizon is being covered by miniature mushroom clouds of an atom bomb which gradually get larger and larger; as if this is not enough of a disaster in itself, the sky is instantly packed with warcraft; bombs are raining down from everywhere and I am looking for my bag as if this is the only activity which can save me from destruction; finding it, I rush into the house yet, no sooner am I inside, than the house becomes a hell of poisonous gas and I cannot breathe; suffocated and almost choked to death, I wake up. I have to establish a metaphysical relationship between the bag and breathing, I think. *Work's Tiring:* Cesare Pavese.

BARTLEBY

Bartleby, as described by Deleuze under the category of fabulation, is one of the best examples of dreaming of people who do not exist, of people to come, all because he is a character who prefers not to produce copies out of originals. In other words, Bartleby is the rejection of a mimetic way of being. This is actually why Melville gives not even one visual clue about Bartleby throughout the whole story. This also explains why we do not have any visual residue of Bartleby in mind when we close our eyes at the end: he is a signifier without a signified. He prefers the rejection of assuming any future identity-to-come: an affirmation of a positive rejection.

ONTO-TERRORISM

According to Adorno and Horkheimer,

> Book XII of the Odyssey tells of the encounter with the Sirens. Their allure is that of losing oneself in the past. [...] But the Sirens' song has not yet been rendered powerless by reduction to the condition of art. [...] Even though the Sirens know all that has happened, they demand the future as the price of that knowledge, and the promise of the happy return is the deception with which the past ensnares the one who longs for it. [...] He knows only two possible ways to escape. One of them he prescribes for his men. He plugs their ears with wax, and they must row with all their strength. [...] The other is the possibility Odysseus, the seigneur who allows the others to labour for themselves, reserves for himself. He listens, but while bound impotently to the mast; the greater the temptation, the more he has his bonds tightened.[1]

While foregrounding the ancients' horror in front of the immediacy of art in the form of possible results that resound from times prehistorical, the Sirens' song also underlines the dangers of the unmediated, or rather, as that very popular term today would have it, the "terror" of the unmediated. In other words, the Sirens' song founds artwork on an ontology of danger and fear; to hear that which precedes art as form comes as a result of a primordial passage. At the origin of all myths there is such a passage from the unformed to the formed: a passage from the

---

1 Theodor Adorno and Max Horkheimer, *Dialectic of Enlightenment,* trans. John Cumming (New York: Continuum, 1989), 32–34.

cosmic cloud of the "*-dividual*" to the organizational force of the "*in-dividual.*" Beneath the unquestionable ontology based on the division of labor of the dialectics of the oppressor and the oppressed lurks the terror of the reversal of this passage.

Art thus becomes what it is by leaving behind the fear, the terror which originally lies at its foundation; form thus transforms deferment into pleasure by means of becoming a mediator to art and by welcoming the terror of destruction to the waiting lounge of fantasy.

> The bonds with which he has irremediably tied himself to practice, also keep the Sirens away from practice: their temptation is neutralized and becomes a mere object of contemplation — becomes art. The prisoner is present at a concert, an inactive eavesdropper like later concertgoers, and his spirited call for liberation fades like applause. Thus the enjoyment of art and manual labour break apart as the world of prehistory is left behind.[2]

From then on, with a desire to overcome its hopelessness, art must console itself with Aesthetics. In spite of the fact that Onto-terrorism is the Artaudesque theatre of violence of the artist and the art-lover, "[t]hey must doggedly sublimate in additional effort the drive that impels to diversion. And so they become practical."[3]

---

2 Ibid., 34.
3 Ibid.

SCULPTURE

One of those pricks says: "But this is not art." I have spent so many years thinking of what distinguishes art from non-art and have eventually reached a point of undecidability, but this prick, without having thought — not even for a single moment — about it, with an empty-set power of imagination tied directly to the transcendental, as if bursting out from a clockwork orange, has made a decision. Actually it is a "mock-punk" event erected against the *Contemporary Istanbul*'s approach to art, yet in sum it is exactly a simulation of ideological misery. Politics has always been your ditch, right; it is either yours or theirs? So is Capital: a sculpture which is a dispositive of *Realpolitik*. There is no place for the political nor the cutupidité neither here nor there. Contemporary art – Aeon = capital conflict n+1.

Fig. 5. "Last Vestiges of the Durée," watercolor, acrylic, pen, pencil, 15 × 20 cm, 2016.

BIRDS, HORSES, INSECTS ...

We are taking a walk on the edge of an abyss opened in kids by their fathers who do not come back home at nights and in a father who failed to join the funeral ceremony of his kids in *Kuşlar Yasına Gider*.[1] Hasan Ali Toptaş[2] never lets us fall into the abyss because he installs an abyss within us by means of his narrative, just as he places a sense of being wasted in *Reckless*.[3] No matter how one struggles to set oneself free from the institution of fatherhood, which fucked up the lives of those who migrated from the countryside to the cities and thus also fucked the integrated lives of the city dwellers, everyone must eventually recount one's own share of the Oedipal. There are no such ludicrous metaphors such as "the red" etc. in the book; construction of the imaginary is so much here and now and with us such that we immediately recognize it. This is Toptaş's genius. Birds, horses, insects, forests, roads, trees go hand in hand to make the narrative possible as much as those who render life impossible for us.

---

1 Hasan Ali Toptaş, *Kuşlar Yasına Gider* (İstanbul: Everest Yayınları, 2016).
2 Hasan Ali Toptaş (1958) is a prominent Turkish novelist and short story writer. He has the reputation of being the Kafka of Turkish literature. His only book available in English is *Heba* (*Reckless*, trans. M. Freely and J. Angliss [London: Bloomsbury, 2013]) and the "reckless" translation turns the book into a funfare of gross mistakes and profound tastelessness.
3 Hasan Ali Toptaş, *Heba* (İstanbul: İletişim Yayınları, 2013).

"PHILOSOPHER"

Some notes on Slavoj Žižek's decision, if he were an American citizen, to vote for Trump.[1]

A philosopher-clone marketed consistently with flags and confetti doesn't need anything more than a Hegel: you add a bit of Lacan on top, and a bit of a watered-down version of Deleuze and there you have a sage who has always been in demand by the media slaves with answers for all their questions. Maintenance of negativity is never achieved with such charlatanism in Hegel and the comprehension of the difficulty of its maintenance requires an exasperatingly close reading of Adorno (*Negative Dialektik*). Although it is a friend of philosophy, sophistication most of the time runs the risk of falling into sophistry.

Hegel failed to be employed by Žižek, that is, the early Hegel of the Jena period during which he contemplated together with the Schlegel brothers, has got nothing to do with a dialectics with absolutes. Žižek is always on the front foot, blending an orthodox Marxism with an ordinary Lacanism to reach the same conclusion each and every time. For example, beneath cultural studies or film studies, there is always the non-locatable signified whose location always already comes to hand even before the discussion begins. He has no tolerance for the free floating signified of Deleuze, but especially of Derrida, which eludes all attempts at being fixed; and this is the reason why his readers

---

1   "Slavoj Žižek Would Vote for Trump," *Žižek.uk*, November 3, 2016, https://zizek.uk/slavoj-zizek-would-vote-for-trump/.

find solutions for every problem as the solution is already posited right from the start.

NEGOTIATIONS

1. The negativity that Deleuze struggles to circumvent has a place in Platonic dialectics where it is not accounted for in a dialectical negativity as in Hegel.

2. Affirmation suggested as positive by Deleuze is relevant only when and where the positive is maintained as an Hegelian negation of the negation.

3. Deleuzian affirmation is at root a non-conceptual negativity which he unavoidably had to tailor in the form of positivity to negate Hegelian dialectics (synthesis/*Aufhebung*).

4. Neither positive vs. negative nor non-being vs. *non*-being can be thought without accounting for *la métaphysique de la présence,* and in order to be able to declare such oppositions unmaintainable, it is necessary to negate, rather than affirm the pseudo-difference which makes this situation possible by means of a non-conceptual negativity.

5. Deleuzian thought calls for an undecidable subject, or a subjectlessness rather than a subject.

6. Non-conceptual negativity has a close affinity with a position of subjectlessness, recounted especially in Deleuze and Guattari's Kafka book[1] in the form of the subjectlessness of schizo-incest and/or bachelor-machines.

---

1 Gilles Deleuze and Félix Guattari, *Kafka: Toward a Minor Literature,* trans. Dana Polan (Minneapolis: University of Minnesota Press, 1986).

ECONOMY, CAPITAL, AND RAPE

In *Difference and Repetition* Deleuze suggests:

"[T]he economic" is never given properly speaking, but rather designates a differential virtuality to be interpreted, always covered over by its forms of actualisation; a theme or "problematic" always covered over by its cases of solution. In short, the economic is the social dialectic itself — in other words, the totality of the problems posed to a given society, or the synthetic and problematising field of that society.[1]

Behind his suggestion is of course Marx's determination in the introduction to his contribution to the *Critique of Political Economy* that "mankind always sets itself only such tasks as it can solve,"[2] which for Deleuze "does not mean that the problems are only apparent or that they are already solved, but, on the contrary, the economic conditions of a problem determine or give rise to the manner in which it finds a solution within the framework of the real relations of the society."[3] So, in Deleuze, the differences, obtaining a quality of virtuality through expelling negativity, turn into the affirmation of each and every difference and consequently the solution is sought in the activation of this virtuality.

---

1 Gilles Deleuze, *Difference and Repetition*, trans. Paul Patton (London and New York: Continuum, 2001), 186.
2 Karl Marx, *A Contribution to the Critique of Political Economy,* trans. S.W. Ryazanskaya (1977; rpt. Marxists.org, 1999), https://www.marxists.org/archive/marx/works/1859/critique-pol-economy/preface.htm.
3 Deleuze, *Difference and Repetition,* 186.

As the dollar gains tremendous momentum these days, the economic problem proper should find a solution in the bankruptcy of the Turkish economy; yet in contrast what is offered to us as the problem is a bill to be passed in parliament — a bill which vindicates the rapist, as it were[4] — as if the bankruptcy of capital is merely a virtuality never to be raped. In both cases, simulation is at work or the negative is being kept in the hands of capital as always. Take a shower sirs, take a shower; if capital goes bankrupt, the virtual differences are already arranged in such a way as to reach a completely different problem.

Civil war is proposed and then withdrawn. Even if the second trauma arrives, it won't make us remember the first one. They will wait for the time when everything will be accepted as it is given out to be. As I said before, all their strife is about concealing the bankruptcy of capital, not surrendering the negative to us.

---

4   In November 2016, the AKP government of Turkey proposed a bill that would liberate a convicted male rapist from a imprisonment, if the rapist agreed to marry the raped.

CHILDREN

Godard said once upon a time that children are treated as political prisoners and Deleuze added that we should take this seriously.

Fig. 6. "Last Vestiges of a Child Not-Yet-Raped," watercolor, acrylic, pen, pencil, 15 × 20 cm, 2016.

PHOTOGRAPH

Art had been able to keep its "onto-terrorist" origin a secret for ages, yet it would get into deep trouble in the nineteenth century. Although it could cover its incessant claim to be unmediated with aesthetics until then, the pangs of a return to formless though still in the form of a form had commenced to call back the ghosts of onto-terrorism into the scene. Jacques Aumont, opposing the materialist theoreticians who locate the origin of the modernist image in the opening of single point Renaisssance perspectivism to muliplicity, argues that at the origin of the photographic and cinematic image lies the difference between "the *ébauche*" and "the *étude*."[1] The ébauche is the detailed draft that the artist draws on the canvas before painting, whereas the étude is the first impression of a scene which the painter scribbles away in immediacy in its transience, in its momentariness. The *étude*, rather than brimming with keen aesthetic concerns, is an attempt to capture the fleeting moment of a subjective experience as it would subsequently be crowned by modernism. At this juncture Classical art's acceptance of form as the mediator collapses and gives way not only to the unmediated, the formless, the momentary but also to a yearning for representing movement much in line with changes in perception—in line with Benjamin's consideration of the daily shocks in a metropolis[2]— occurring in the metropolitan subject. It all seems as if it is

---

1 Jacques Aumont, "The Variable Eye, or the Mobilization of the Gaze," in *The Image in Dispute: Art and Cinema in the Age of Photography*, ed. Dudley Andrew (Austin: University of Texas Press, 1997), 231–58.
2 Walter Benjamin, "On Some Motifs in Baudelaire," in *Illuminations: Essays and Reflections,* trans. Harry Zohn, ed. Hannah Arendt (New York: Schocken, 1968), 155–200, at 165.

a matter of time now for art to reclaim its power to affect without a mediator. Baudelaire's *The Painter of Modern Life* (1863) in this sense is a paean to modern life where he concentrates on movement and speed, with Constantin Guys in view: "Our strange artist expresses both the gestures and attitudes, be they solemn or grotesque, of human beings and their luminous explosion in space."[3] Explosion? Without doubt, it is a reference to photography's capacity to capture, to represent life in its luminosity and movement, that is, the magnesium powder which is the basic element of flash that will hit the market in the 1880s.

All this points to the fact that by the time Niépce produced the first photograph in 1826, the photographic perception of the world had already been well rooted in the art world, as the introduction of *études* into halls of exhibition bears witness. The newspaper delivery boys who discuss the bicycle races leaning on their bicycles are yet unaware of the things to happen to Benjamin in the near future but they keep enjoying the "information" made possible by the newspaper pages, illustrated first by lithographs and then by photographs, to capture, to represent the "reality" of the events in their immediacy which art, wishing to reunite with the Sirens' Song, had yearned for hopelessly until that day. The terror of explosion, traversing the onto-terrorism brought along with immediacy, submits the photographic image first to the service of the newspaper, and then to the cinema and the media, and re-contaminates the arts with the deception of being unmediated — zombie-art — with the invention of installation and video art as repudiated by Virilio.[4]

---

3 Charles Baudelaire, "The Painter in Modern Life," in *The Painter of Modern Life and Other Essays,* trans. Jonathan Mayne (London: Phaidon Press, 1995), 1–40, at 35.
4 Paul Virilio, *Art and Fear,* trans. Julie Rose (London: Continuum, 2004).

OLD AGE

"The tragedy of old age is not that one is old, but that one is young" — Oscar Wilde.[1]

---

[1] Oscar Wilde, *The Picture of Dorian Gray* (London: Penguin Classics, 2000), 222.

NEGATIVITY

What we predicted for the world in the 80s has become the negation of negation in the hands of a few charlatans today — what they call democracy is what for ages we have known as fascism. It is not only about emptying the content of concepts; the attack comes from deeper levels. As we were dealing *à la* Blanchot with double negation,[1] that is, with the rejection of a proper language which renders possible the object and the object as concept in turn, they have transformed the double negation into affirmation. This is what they beat us with, by rendering the negative invisible.

---

1 Maurice Blanchot, *The Infinite Conversation,* trans. Susan Hanson (Minneapolis: University of Minnesota Press, 2008), 66–80.

CUTUPIDITÉ[1]

1. Cutupidité is a discontinuous plane of consistency resisting any plane of immanence.

2. Cutupidité is non-organic rhizome made of multi-dimensional, infinite cuts where each cut lays bare an unique event which cannot be repeated.

3. Cutupidité is the art of hyperbole where each negation of space triggers an aerial fugue, completely non-traceable.

4. Cutupidité is not serial but aerial; actually it is an aerial fugue, which, soaring above the surface of the rhizome, traverses each and every cut inflicted on it.

5. Cutupidité is somnambulism; or a hypnosis without a hypnotist.

6. Cutupidité is to become-spectral without coordinates; it is not becoming-immaterial but becoming-gaseous.

7. Cutupidité is the Cotard delusion: *le délire de négation* — to demolish the dimensional with a discontinuous multiplic-

---

[1] I coined and developed the concept of "cutupidité" in my essay, "Cutupidité: Devenir-Radicalement-Stupide," *Revue Chimères* 81 (2014): 111–19. The English version was published as "Cutupidité: Becoming-Radically-Stupid," *Rhizomes* 28 (Spring 2015), http://rhizomes.net/issue28/aracagok/index.html.

ity of dimensions so as to open up a psychasthenic[2] *nonground*.

8. Cutupidité is *contigentia absoluta* (potentiality without will): a zero state of wanting; failure before failure.

9. Cutupidité is the affirmation of paranoia as a form of extreme wakefulness.

10. Cutupidité is suicidal in content and disastrous in form.

11. Cutupidité is the smoke of the cliché and the last breath of wisdom.

12. Cutupidité is knowing all styles but appropriating none.

13. Cutupidité is the *instinct d'abandon* vs. *élan vital*.

14. Cutupidité is infinite dividuation.

15. Cutupidité is done with anthropocentrism.

16. Cutupidité is the incorporation of *stupidité*.

---

[2] The surrealist zoologist Roger Caillois describes this term which he borrowed from Pierre Janet as a desire to get lost in space. See Roger Caillois, "Mimicry and Legendary Psychasthenia," in *The Edge of Surrealism: A Roger Callois Reader*, ed. Claudeine Frank (Durham: Duke University Press, 2003), 89–106.

ANIMALS

When it is understood that animals are constituted as singularities, humans will give up making documentaries on animals.

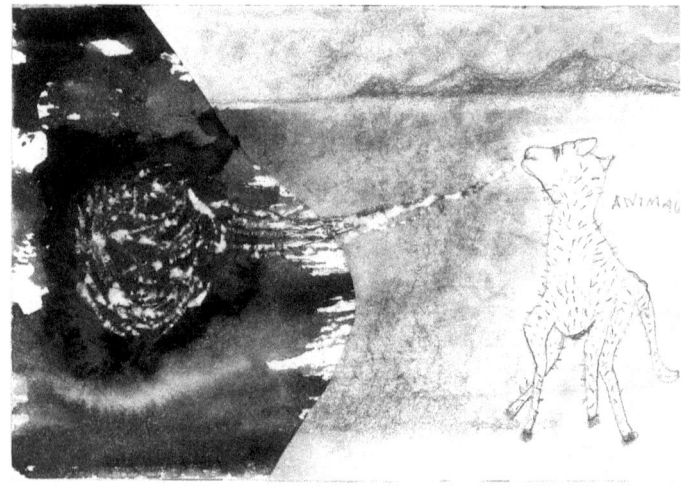

Fig. 7. "Last Vestiges of Becoming-Animal," watercolor, acrylic, pen, pencil, 15 × 20 cm, 2016.

CHAMPIONS OF AFFIRMATION

Cinematic works express themselves in the field of visibility like anything else; and the perception of expression is realized on a plane of mutual movement and change. Therefore, neither one single expression has one single thing that is expressed nor one single perception is exactly the same with one another. Yet all this does not lead to relativity as the differences between various perceptions do not mean that each difference is as relevant as the other. Relativity is a moment when difference is always affirmed and thus eventually rendered negative by being affirmed; there is difference but since each difference is rendered equally relevant as another, there is no room left for difference because all differences are now equalized. The difference of Deleuzian difference must be sought in the fact that here each difference, negating one another, leads us to a plane of competing differences: a competition where the winner is never announced and equalization is constantly negated. The champions of affirmation surrendered not only the power of Deleuzian philosophy but also the power of the negative to capital today. Capital, which has always welcomed the slackening of affirmation by the force of negation, has never tolerated nor will ever tolerate difference as such. How long will we allow the manipulation of the negative by capital?

PARTISANS

Partisans, who invest all their energy in the maintenance of this order, are advertising blockheads, tv series casts, artists whose high beams are always on, writers who think literature is all about writing a novel, academics of bureaucratic resentment, pop-music assholes of one-rhythm-double-refrain, men of marriage, women of marriage, the lipless who think to write poetry is to get emotional, lovers of work without production, fools of the mimetic, nano-fascist dead-heads.

METAPHYSICS

It wasn't like this before, right? Now you look at the TV channels, and there is a procession of stupid faces, made duller by a failed modernity, tied to a transcendental voice — obedient servants. You can say that it's all the same everywhere, and it was like this before yet nobody would have guessed that after the '70s and '80s metaphysics would hit back, so profoundly resentful. Nietzsche had warned us so particularly: he heard the footsteps of the Führer ages ago when he said that the death of the God shouldn't mean the creation of another god out of human beings. Should the reason for the transformation of modernity into dictatorships almost everywhere today be sought in the translation of metaphysics into the human by means of modernity or in the manipulation of high modernism's dream of a laicist world into a human-god with the aid of nano-technologies?

STUPIDITY

In the last chapter of the *Dialectic of Enlightenment,* Adorno and Horkheimer claim that "Stupidity is a wound."[3] This wound is carved out by the first question of the child or the suppression of questioning about the first. From then on, although it gets calloused, insensitive, congealed and invisible, this is the source of stupidity. One wonders where this stupidity will reach as long as the negativity that silenced the child remains the monopoly of Neanderthal capitalism.

---

3   Theodor Adorno and Max Horkheimer, *Dialectic of Enlightenment,* trans. John Cumming (New York: Continuum, 1989), 256–58.

ZOMBIE-ART

In other words, no painting, no photograph, no film, no piece of writing can tell it better than this photograph[1] that the media works on the principle of Image Explosion. When photography, which made it possible to capture the fleeting moment, merged the terror of the real with the newspaper, art had died and the media, seizing art's centuries long claim to the unmediated, condemned the reader/spectator to the exitless prisonhouse of onto-terrorism. Even the suicide of Walter Benjamin, which he committed upon hearing the rumors about the Nazis' advent to Portbou could not wake human beings from the dream that the unmediated will endow mankind with infinity. With this move, art as we know it, that is, classical art, which requires distance and contemplation, dies and zombie-art takes hold of the scene. Without obliterating the hope that we can regain the infinite by returning the finitude of thought to the transcendental, in other words, without overcoming Kantian transcendental empiricism, this world will not come to an end; no matter how immortal you declare yourself to be, the infinite will always transcend you and, stealing the negativity of the world from you, it will always hide from you the fact that the Explosion is a matter of the dervishism of Capital.

---

1 The photograph I am referring to is the one taken when the Russian Ambassador to Turkey, Andrei Karlov, was assasinated during a visit to an exhibition in Ankara in 2016, http://time.com/4606972/russian-ambassador-karlov-turkey-assasination-photo-burhan-ozbilici/. I reworked this photo in one of my artworks included in the book, cf. Fig 8. "Last Vestiges of Mimesis."

Fig. 8. "Last Vestiges of Mimesis"
watercolor, acrylic, pen, pencil, 15 × 20 cm, 2016.

MIMESIS

Mimesis means to mistake the rustling of the leaves for the waves breaking on the shore while walking in a forest: not to end up in such a deduction is the indication of a desire to reach from the zero point of brain to brain-1, though in vain.

ADORNO: NEGATIVE DIALECTICS[1]

To read *Negative Dialectics*[2] once again, armed with some unripe thoughts about "non-conceptual negativity," might point to some subterranean passages from Adorno to Deleuze on the basis of a negativity which is not yet conceptual. In Adorno, difference is understood as a way to preserve contradictions within the context of a non-identical dialectic where subject and object are not reconciled and thus the prepondorance of the subject is not guaranteed. Negativity has an extremely important role in this process, especially in the activity of the rejection of such a reconciliation whereby the throne of the subject is demolished, not in order to replace the object as the next occupier of the throne, but to put an end to the hierarchy between subject and object. Given this, which I will develop in detail below, for the moment let me just suggest that there is here a reverse relationship between Adorno's negativite dialectic and the one Deleuze discusses in *Difference and Repetition* with regard to Plato's dialectic, one which works on a non-dialectical negativity and which has not gone Hegelian yet. Despite the fact that at this stage what Adorno and Deleuze have in common is only a strange negativity, I should stress straight away that it is not the negativity which has been detected by the Speculative Realists

---

1   Noys claims that a possible negativity in Deleuze is sacrificed to positivity thereby erasing the possibility of a subject or an agent in thought. Yet what kind of a negativity is it and why has it been rejected by Deleuze? Although this negativity is rejected by Deleuze because it is nonceptual and always acts as a shadow of thought, non-conceptual negativity, as we will discover soon via Adorno, can be understood in different ways.
2   Theodor W. Adorno, *Negative Dialectics*, trans. E.B. Ashton (London: Routledge, 1990).

in Deleuze, who has thus been criticized for not putting it into action in conformity with a political programme.[3] If Deleuze himself did not do so, could it be because of the non-conceptuality of this negativity which would always escape from the programmatic, remaining negative even after the negation of the negation, and according to which the primacy of the positive could never be maintained? Could it also be because of this unmaintainable primacy of this positivity, which acts not as a negativity that prevents the reconciliation of contradictions but as a strange kind of positivity whose function is to preserve differences and to reject/negate the identical and synthesis?

In order to understand this strange positivity, we must look further into chapters on negativity in *Negative Dialektik*. The war Adorno wages is first of all against the conceptual because humanity has conceptualized and consequently dominated all of Nature by giving preponderance to the subject (idealist) as against the object and overlooked the non-conceptual, which not only stands side by side with the conceptual but also remains always as a residue in it. For Adorno, thought is in the first place negation, fundamentally the negation of the "unmediated" which is imposed upon us by hegemonic discourses, the negation of thought's Hegelian positivism. If it is the main duty of philosophy to determine the non-conceptual in the conceptual, the primal task of this determination is to give the lie to the synthetic identities in this thought in order to lead it to the non-identical. Although the conceptual is one of the basic elements of dialectical logic, the non-conceptual has always played an essential part in its coming into being or in its acquisition of signification. The route of conceptualization which always goes from the noumenal to the phenomenal in Kant can only be reversed by negative dialectics and the strait-jacket forced by the conceptual on the conceptual can be cast aside only in this way.

---

3   See, for example, Benjamin Noys's chapters on Derrida and Deleuze in *Persistence of the Negative* (Edinburgh: Edinburgh University Press, 2010), 23–66.

Negative dialectic means "to think in contradictions, for the sake of the contradiction once experienced in the thing, and against that contradiction. A contradiction in reality, it is a contradiction against reality."[4] At this point, Adorno is elaborating a dialectic that is completely non-Hegelian, all because he does not deduce an identity from the difference between and object and its concept, and, hence, poses a profound doubt as to the availability of identity as such. In a chapter entitled, "Disintegration of Logic,"[5] Adorno claims that there is nothing that can be obtained from thought in the name of the positive because the structure of negativity forces all identities to disintegrate, building up a structure of its own. "What would be different has not begun as yet"[6] because the concept of a concept has become problematic: which is just to say that Hegelian dialectic cannot be so easily maintained because neither the positive obtained as a result of a second negation of difference seen as contradiction nor the difference necessary for the realization of synthesis can be maintained in face of the impossibility of reducing the negative to the conceptual. It is only after all identity is forced to the point of disintegration that difference will arise on the horizon. Negativity forces thought to difference, the only available way of maintaining difference, and it can be realized only when negativity is saved from the yoke of the conceptual. On the other hand, it is not to be thought at this juncture that negativity produces a pure, unmediated non-conceptuality. If Hegelian dialectic is prone to severe criticism by Adorno because it stretches from the non-conceptual to the conceptual on the basis of a one-way-ticket, Adorno's negative dialectic is a return ticket to lay bare the non-conceptual, the non-identical in the concept: here there's nothing which is unmediated, unrepresented.

---

4   Adorno, *Negative Dialectics*, 145.
5   Ibid., 144–46.
6   Ibid., 145.

LAUGHTER

In a world where Nietzschean laughter is transformed into neurotic expressionism, the border separating the Freudian conscious from the unconscious has disappeared and we have fallen prey to the intra-conscious: if today laughter bursts out only where joy has been made impossible, the bodily assemblage which made laughter burst has been damaged in one way or another, giving way to a new type of human being. One who looks at the world from within the intra-conscious does not know that one's laughter is actually a vomiting inside and that one has created a crypt out of oneself. One bursts into laughter now not in order to ridicule the world but to be ridiculed.

NEW YEAR

I do not think journalism has a tremendous impact on life. What is it to receive the news? It is the objectivization of the Aristotleian "now" without which neither past nor future can be perceived. In other words, it is as if the concept of "now" cannot be experienced without mediation, without the media. Hence, the organization of the newspapers and the media into the sophistry that we are accustomed to call Democracy, based allegedly on the principle of distribution of equal rights. Journalism as the safety valve of a system of administration with inequality as its founding principle, that is, the equal distribution of inequality, is a false negativity constituted by political power to consolidate and prolong its hegemony. The possibility of the return of the spectres of Marx is thus reduced to a certain programme and the journalist risen from the dead from the underground world of Orpheus becomes the touchstone of the inexpressibility of the real. The new year will never arrive as long as the news fail to become the "event."

SHOCK: 2017

During the last week of 2016, the media incessantly broadcast news of snow approaching Istanbul; the snow is on its way, the snow will be taking the city, hey snow, disaster snow — we were alerted to an approaching disaster, as it were; then all of a sudden power outages hit the city with no clear explanation from the municipality, accompanied by Islamist attacks on Santa Claus; entering the new year with anxieties about possible — unforeseeable — power cuts, finally the real bomb exploded in Reina — we are falling victim to the intra-conscious via such manipulations; *onto-logie* transformed into onto-terrorism, the daily shocks of the nineteenth-century Paris of Baudelaire multiplied ten thousand times.

ANTIDOTE

Antidote is a negativity which we forgot how to use: in careless hands it can easily turn into poison.

CARAVAGGIO

Or, we can read Caravaggio's "Judith and Holofernes" as Mieke Bal did many years ago,[1] within a logic of "quotation" in the context of art history, that is, in order to reach an anachronistic feminism finding a point of departure in semiotic structures. Yet none of these readings explain why we feel so horrified in front of this painting. In order to save her people from the siege, Judith cuts the head of Holofernes, the head of the occupying forces, and, as if to stress Judith's setting free of a negativity both in historical and visual terms, the blood imagined to gush from the neck of her victim turn into threads that Holofernes hopelessly pulls at out of his neck. Although the negativity that Judith forgot a long time ago has been put into action, what takes place is also due to Holofernes' falling prey to his own habit of domesticating any type of negativity by way of negation. The threads of blood, instead of forming an unsmooth surface in reaction to the disturbance inflicted by the habit of Holofernes' ephemeral negation of negation, undo the knots in the canvas's constitution to lay bare before our eyes the stitches of the supposed synthesis. The awaited reconciliation is not realized; the negative remains negative by the sweeping force of negation; the horror we are driven to before the painting emanates not from the representation of a bloody scene but from the uncanny implication that even art would dissolve in face of negativity that is strong enough.

---

[1] Mieke Bal, "Seeing Signs: The Use of Semiotics for the Understanding of Visual Art," in *The Subjects of Art History: Historical Objects in Contemporary Perspectives*, eds. Mark A. Cheetham, Michael Ann Holly, and Keith Moxey (New York: Cambridge University Press, 1998), 74–93.

What Caravaggio teaches us is that art is capable of dissolving impossible situations by employing negativity as an antidote to poison, if we are ready to sacrifice the "subjectile" a bit.

REPETITION

If you repeat the metaphors a thousand times you end up in fascism;

If you repeat them ten thousand times you end up in micro-fascism;

If you repeat them a hundred thousand times you end up in nano-fascism

— this is how reality is constructed.

Fig. 9. "Last Vestiges of I Am Sick of This World," watercolor, acrylic, pen, pencil, 15 × 20 cm, 2016.

SURRENDER

In *Negative Dialektik,* Adorno claimed that Husserl and Bergson could not save thought from idealism; that they could not theorize a subject/object distinction without absolutizing the subject. Without doubt, it was a position maintained by an epistemological ontology which could easily be overcome by a critique of metaphysics by Deleuze or Derrida. On the other hand, Adorno had another thing in mind with respect to the negativity of the subject. Although the difference between the subject and the object could be maintained ontologically, it was impossible to absolutize this difference due to the negativity involved in the concept of the subject. The problem with this distinction became apparent not only when the subject started to dominate the world by manipulating its negativity but also when it surrendered its negativity to the object so as to be affirmed by it and thus, in turn, when it affirmed the object by means of its own negativity.

The necessity to rethink negativity still lingers on.

SOMNAMBULIST SITUATIONIST MANIFESTO

"Why"ing, not in order to get ready-made responses to daily media bombardements, and media intellectualisms, Somnambulist Situationists aim at miraculating a sleepwalker's strategy to re-consider the Situationist Internationalist's texts towards an un-negotiable, short-circuiting, non-identitarian, and especially a critically perverted position.

How can we hypnotise the Father, or Hegel? Or better, how can we maintain a drowsy-Hegel, not quite awake yet? What if the father is hypnotised so that he can be made to confess his trauma? Isn't it timely to radicalise *détournement* as a way of producing the *un-Gestalt* of a WHATEVER-IMAGE?

How can we hypnotise the Father, or Freud, so that psychoanalysis itself is forced to lead the life of a somnambulist? Imagine somnambulist "citizens" who cross the borders for schizo-incesting towards a homosexual-effusion … bachelor-machines.

The undecidable is what lies between one's eyelids.

NON-CONCEPTUAL NEGATIVITY

Is difference in Deleuze an unmediated difference? At this juncture, it is important to stress that the dialectic criticized by Deleuze is the Hegelian one. Moreover, it should be added that when the Platonic dialectic is in particular prioritized over the Hegelian one, Deleuzian thought gets much closer to Adorno, especially in the context of the non-conceptual and the non-identical. According to Deleuze:

> It is not difference which presupposes opposition but opposition which presupposes difference, and far from resolving difference by tracing it back to a foundation, opposition betrays and distorts it. Our claim is not only that difference in itself is not 'already' contradiction, but that it cannot be reduced or traced back to contradiction, since the latter is not more but less profound than difference. On what condition is difference traced or projected on to a flat space? Precisely when it has been forced into a previously established identity, when it has been placed on the slope of the identical which makes it reflect or desire identity, and necessarily takes it where identity wants it to go — namely, into the negative.[1]

Why does Deleuze reject this negativity? It is all because in Hegel the negative, considering its concept and its object as identical, reduces the two down to the same and with conceptuality and representability thus produced, synthesis, which is to appear only at the end, has at the beginning already been decided.

---

1   Gilles Deleuze, *Difference and Repetition*, trans. Paul Patton (London and New York: Continuum, 2001), 51.

On the other hand, difference when reduced to identity disappears immediately because it is surrendered to representation, which reduces everything down to the same and the identical. It is impossible to think difference in itself when it is subjected to the protocols of representation.[2] Yet there is a way of thinking difference in itself without representing it, without surrendering it to identity, without rendering it mediated; and it is only possible to think difference without conceptualizing it. And all this can only be achieved by the paradoxical element we mentioned earlier.

There are two possible conclusions which can be derived from this discussion:

1. Since it leads to Hegelian synthesis, Deleuze does not indulge in representation in so far as difference is concerned; he is convinced that unmediated thought cannot be maintained by the negation of difference but by Nietzschean affirmation. The paradoxical element will empty capital of all its signification due to its non-locatability obtained by double affirmation, yet right at this extremely critical point, Deleuze seems to be unaware of the fact that his preference for unmediated thought or the power of affirmation of this thought is maintained by being subjected to the double negation of capital itself. You are free to affirm as long as you let yourself be doubly negated by capital. Such a position, of course, plays into the hands of the Speculative Realists who insist on a philosophy of the subject in the face of the "*non*."[3]

---

2 Ibid., 262.
3 Speculative Realists' insistence on the "non" finds its point of departure in François Laruelle's philosophy. For his positioning of the subject within a seemingly new and radical perspective, see François Laruelle, *Principles of Non-Philosophy*, trans. N. Rubczak and A.P. Smith (London: Bloomsbury, 2017).

2. Re-read Deleuze in the light of Adorno where negativity is rendered non-conceptual. If behind Deleuze's affirmative thought, as Adorno would have it, there still remains a negativity even after the negation of the negation, it is so because it is a nonceptual negativity resistant to being reduced to a programme. What would be the implications of reading the positive obtained under such circumstances — a positive which can no longer preserve its primacy — both as the negative which does not allow for the reconciliation of contradictions, and also as the positive which preserves difference as difference by rejecting the same and synthesis? Isn't there a shared nonceptuality, or rather a non-conceptual negativity, at the origin of such a strange positive, a positive that is condemned to be determined by its shadow and the negative as a residue? Re-read Deleuze in the light of Adorno where negativity is rendered non-conceptual. If behind Deleuze's affirmative thought, as Adorno would have it, there still remains a negativity even after the negation of the negation, it is so because it is a nonceptual negativity resistant to being reduced to a programme. What would be the implications of reading the positive obtained under such circumstances — a positive which can no longer preserve its primacy — both as the negative which does not allow for the reconciliation of contradictions, and also as the positive which preserves difference as difference by rejecting the same and synthesis? Isn't there a shared nonceptuality, or rather a non-conceptual negativity, at the origin of such a strange positive, a positive that is condemned to be determined by its shadow and the negative as a residue?

Fig. 10. "Last Vestiges of a Rhizomatic Life," watercolor, acrylic, pen, pencil, 15 × 20 cm, 2016.

BIBLIOGRAPHY

Abraham, Nicholas and Maria Török. *The Wolfman's Magic Word: A Cryptonomy*. Translated by Nicholas T. Rand. Minneapolis: University of Minnesota Press, 1986.

———. *The Shell and the Kernel: Renewals of Psychoanalysis, Volume 1*. Translated by Nicholas T. Rand. Chicago: The University of Chicago Press, 1994.

Adorno, Theodor. *Negative Dialectics*. Translated by E.B. Ashton. London: Routledge, 1990.

———, Else Frenkel-Brunswik, Daniel Levinson, and Nevitt Sanford, *The Authoritarian Personality*. New York: Harper & Row, 1950.

——— and Max Horkheimer. *Dialectic of Enlightenment*. Translated by John Cumming. London: Verso, 1989.

Aracagök, Zafer. *Atopological Trilogy: Deleuze and Guattari*. Brooklyn: punctum books, 2015.

———. "Cutupidité: Becoming-Radically-Stupid." *Rhizomes* 28 (Spring 2015). http://rhizomes.net/issue28/aracagok/index.html.

———. "Cutupidité: Devenir-Radicalement-Stupide." *Revue Chimères* 81 (February 2014): 111-19. DOI: 10.3917/chime.081.0111.

———. *Desonance: Desonating (with) Deleuze*. Saarbrücken: VDM Verlag, 2009.

Aumont, Jacques. "The Variable Eye, or the Mobilization of the Gaze." In *The Image in Dispute: Art and Cinema in the Age of Photography*, edited by Dudley Andrew, 231–58. Austin: University of Texas Press, 1997.

Bal, Mieke. "Seeing Signs: The Use of Semiotics for the Understanding of Visual Art." In *The Subjects of Art History:*

Historical Objects in Contemporary Perspectives, edited by Mark A. Cheetham, Michael Ann Holly, and Keith Moxey, 74–93. New York: Cambridge University Press, 1998.

Baudelaire, Charles. *The Painter of Modern Life and Other Essays.* Translated by Jonathan Mayne. London: Phaidon Press, 1995.

Benjamin, Walter. "On Some Motifs in Baudelaire." In *Illuminations: Essays and Reflections,* translated by Harry Zohn, edited by Hannah Arendt, 155–200. New York: Schocken, 1968.

Blanchot, Maurice. *The Infinite Conversation.* Translated by Susan Hanson. Minneapolis: University of Minnesota Press, 2008.

Borges, Jorge Luis. "On Exactitude in Science." In *Collected Fictions.* Translated by Andrew Hurley, 325. London: Penguin Books, 1999.

Caillois, Roger. "Mimicry and Legendary Psychasthenia." In *The Edge of Surrealism: A Roger Callois Reader,* edited by Claudeine Frank, 89–106. Durham: Duke University Press, 2003.

Celan, Paul. "Fugue of Death." In *Selected Poems,* translated by Michael Hamburger and Christopher Middleton, 33–34. Harmondsworth: Penguin Books, 1972.

Deleuze, Gilles. "How Do We Recognize Structuralism." In *Desert Islands and Other Texts 1953–1974,* edited by David Lapoujade, translated by Michael Taormina, 170–92. New York: Semiotext(e), 2004.

———. *Difference and Repetition.* Translated by Paul Patton. London and New York: Continuum, 2001.

———. "Literature and Life". Translated by Daniel W. Smith. *Critical Inquiry* 23, no. 2 (Winter, 1997): 225–30. https://www.jstor.org/stable/1343982.

———. *The Logic of Sense.* Translated by M. Lester and C. Stivale. London: Continuum, 2003.

——— and Félix Guattari. *Kafka: Toward a Minor Literature.* Translated by Dana Polan. Minneapolis: University of Minnesota Press, 1986

——— and Félix Guattari. *A Thousand Plateaus: Capitalism and Schizophrenia*. Translated by Brian Massumi. Minneapolis: University of Minnesota Press, 1987.

Griffiths, Mark D. "Dead Strange: A Beginner's Guide to Cotard's Syndrome." *Psychology Today,* October 14, 2014. https://www.psychologytoday.com/us/blog/in-excess/201410/dead-strange.

Hattenstone, Simon. "Seven Rounds with Aki Kaurismäki." *The Guardian,* April 4, 2012. https://www.theguardian.com/film/2012/apr/04/aki-kaurismaki-le-havre-interview.

Howell, F. Clark. "The Evolutionary Significance of Variation and Varieties of 'Neanderthal' Man." *The Quarterly Review of Biology* 32, no. 4 (1957): 330–47. https://www.jstor.org/stable/2816956.

Kleist, Heinrich von. *The Marquise of O— and Other Stories*. Edited and translated by David Luke and Nigel Reeves. New York: Penguin Books, 1978.

———. *Michael Kohlhaas*. Translated by Martin Greenberg. Brooklyn: Melville House, 2005.

Lacoue-Labarthe, Philippe. *Musica Ficta: Figures of Wagner.* Translated by Felicia McCarren. Stanford: Stanford University Press, 1994.

——— and Jean-Luc Nancy. *The Literary Absolute: The Theory of Literature in German Romanticism.* Translated by Philip Barnard and Cheryl Lester. New York: SUNY Press, 1988.

Laruelle, François. *Principles of Non-Philosophy*. Translated by N. Rubczak and A.P. Smith. London: Bloomsbury, 2017.

Lucretius, *De Rerum Natura (The Nature of Things)*. Translated by David R. Slavitt. Berkeley: University of California Press, 2008.

Marx, Karl. *A Contribution to the Critique of Political Economy*. Translated by S.W. Ryazanskaya. 1977; rpt. Marxists.org, 1999. https://www.marxists.org/archive/marx/works/1859/critique-pol-economy/preface.htm.

Noys, Benjamin. *The Persistence of the Negative*. Edinburgh: Edinburgh University Press, 2010.

Sherif Xenoph Ibn el Somnambulist Situationists Constantinople. *I Want to Be a Suicide Bomber.* San Francisco: Little Black Cart Books, 2013.

Spivak, Gayatri. "Terror: A Speech after 9-11," *Boundary 2* 31, no. 2 (2004): 81–111. DOI: 10.1215/01903659-31-2-81.

Toptaş, Hasan Ali. *Heba*. İstanbul: İletişim Yayınları, 2013.

———. *Kuşlar Yasına Gider.* İstanbul: Everest Yayınları, 2016.

———. *Reckless.* Translated by M. Freely and J. Angliss. London: Bloomsbury, 2013.

Virilio, Paul. *Art and Fear.* Translated by Julie Rose. London: Continuum, 2004.

Wilde, Oscar. *The Picture of Dorian Gray*. London: Penguin Classics, 2000.

"W. dreams, like Phaedrus, of an army of thinker-friends, thinker-lovers. He dreams of a thought-army, a thought-pack, which would storm the philosophical Houses of Parliament. He dreams of Tartars from the philosophical steppes, of thought-barbarians, thought-outsiders. What distance would shine in their eyes!"

— Lars Iyer

www.ingramcontent.com/pod-product-compliance
Lightning Source LLC
Chambersburg PA
CBHW051131160426
43195CB00014B/2427